Character Education:

A Primer for Teachers

Edward F. DeRoche
and
Mary M. Williams

ARGUS COMMUNICATIONS

For information:

Argus Communications
400 W. Bethany Drive, Suite 110
Allen, TX 75013
1-800-860-6762
Fax 1-800-243-5299
www.argus.com

Printed in the U.S.A.

10 9 8 7 6 5 4 3 2 1

ISBN: 1-58953-001-2

Contents

About the Authors

Edward F. DeRoche joined the University of San Diego School of Education as Dean in 1979 and returned to the faculty as professor and co-director of the International Center for Character Education in 1998. He received his Bachelor's degree from the University of Maine and a M.Ed. degree from Eastern Connecticut State University. He also earned M.A. and Ph.D. degrees from the University of Connecticut.

Ed was an elementary and junior high school teacher and principal and a member of a public school board of education and has served on several private school boards. He has been past president of the California State Association of Teacher Educators and a member of the California Commission on Teacher Credentialing. He served as a member of the Commission on Character Education for the Association of Teacher Educators.

He is a consultant, speaker, evaluator, author, teacher trainer, and recipient of several awards. Besides teaching courses and conducting workshops on character education, he has published more than fifty articles in education journals and many articles in daily newspapers.

Ed's published books include:

Creative Problem-Solving Techniques for Teachers and Students
Real World Reading Activities for Teachers and Students (co-authored)
Project Update: The Newspaper in the Elementary and Junior High School Classroom
The Newspaper: A Reference Book for Teachers and Librarians
400 Group Games and Activities for Teaching Math (co-authored)
How School Administrators Solve Problems
A Complete Guide to Administering School Services (co-authored)
Public Speaking Handbook for School Administrators
An Administrator's Guide for Evaluating School Programs and Personnel (two editions)
Character Matters: Using Newspapers to Teach Values

Mary M. Williams received a B.S. degree in elementary education from the State University of New York (SUNY), Plattsburgh; an M.S. in reading K–12 from SUNY, Albany; and an Ed.D. in Educational Leadership: Curriculum, Instruction, and Supervision from Boston University. She is currently a Professor of Education at the University of San Diego, where she is also a co-founder and co-director of the International Center for Character Education. Mary is a member of the Committee of Credentials for the California Commission on Teacher Credentialing. She is past chair of the National Commission on Character Education (1997–2000).

Mary has been a K–12 teacher, a reading specialist, a curriculum coordinator, a staff developer, a teacher educator, a program evaluator, and on-line course instructor. She conducts regional and national workshops and makes keynote presentations in character development, ethical/diversity issues and leadership in education, case-based pedagogy, literacy, technology and on-line learning, and authentic assessment.

Mary has published numerous articles, including:

"Actions Speak Louder Than Words: How Students View Character Education," *Educational Leadership* (1993)

"Leadership in Character Education: A Framework for Teaching Values and Ethics," *Education International* (2000)

"Models of Character Education: Perspectives and Developmental Issues," *Journal of Humanistic Counseling, Education and Development* (2000)

In addition, Mary is co-editor of *Character Education: The Foundation of Teacher Education, the Report of the National Commission on Character Education* (1999, Character Education Partnership).

Ed and Mary have co-authored two texts on character education:
Educating Hearts and Minds: A Comprehensive Character Education Framework (two editions published by Corwin Press, 1998 and 2001)
Character Education: A Guide for School Administrators (Scarecrow Press, 2001)

Acknowledgements

Ed DeRoche

Teaching is an art and a science. It is a craft and a performance. It is discovering and learning. It is exhilarating and exhausting. It's about relationships and collaborations. All of these come to mind as I acknowledge those who have guided me on my teaching journey.

To Andy Goulis, who was my mentor during my first year of teaching.

To Alice, Pauline, Shirley, Stan, Fred, and all the other teachers—too many to mention—who guided me through my years of school administration.

To Jack Lester, who proved to me that you don't have to be professionally trained to be a good teacher.

To Jacqueline, my wife, the teacher!

To Diane and Carolyn, my oldest and youngest daughters, teachers both, who are examples of what good character educators are all about.

To my university colleagues—Bob Norberg, Bob Craig, Erika Gierl, and Jack Mulhern—who taught me to think, to write, and to make the transition from teaching children to teaching adults.

And to Mary Williams, who, after I thought I knew all about teaching, opened up new doors, offered new challenges, sparked new ideas, and renewed an excitement for teaching and learning.

Mary Williams

In 1985, I went on a search to find answers to questions about effective teaching. I wanted to know why students behaved for one teacher and not another. I wanted to know how to inspire diverse learners. I needed to understand why some teachers thought they were doing a good job teaching values and prosocial behavior to students but really were not effective. I began the search at Boston University School of Education, where I worked with Kevin Ryan to find some answers. I developed curriculum, studied and practiced teaching strategies, observed students in different contexts, learned about the research conducted in educational psychology about how students learn, and researched effective schooling practices. I read, discussed, talked, observed, reflected, and then prepared, presented, wrote, gave workshops, and developed courses. Over the years, I have uncovered some answers to the questions, and I share them with you in this book.

I want to thank all the teachers I have observed and worked with over the years who have been models of the guiding principles, strategies, and techniques described in this book. I thank all my students who challenged me to find ways to help them learn.

I want to give a special thanks to my parents, John and Olga Williams, who were my first teachers; my stepdaughter, Erica, who makes miracles happen with some of the most difficult-to-teach students; and my husband, Richard, who continues to help me learn new things every day.

Mary and Ed dedicate this book to their graduate and undergraduate students who are preparing to be teachers and to "Character Education" master's students at the University of San Diego, who continually ask those pesky questions, "Why?" "How come?" "Why not?" and "What if?" We want to thank the University of San Diego and the School of Education for their generous support of our work, and special thanks to our Dean, Paula Cordeiro and our graduate fellows, Jenny Ferrone and Ginger Blackman.

Introduction

Schools are an important indicator of the well-being of our democratic society. They remind us of the values that must be passed on to young people in order for them to think critically; to participate in decisions that affect their lives; and to transform inequities that close down democratic social relationships.

Gene Carter, ASCD Conference, Israel,
September 21, 1999

Much has been written about character education. In fact, schools and school districts across the United States and in other countries as well, are responding to the public's concern about the behavior of children and youth. This primer on character education reflects our experiences working with teachers, administrators, counselors, parents, and civic leaders. They, like you, have questions about how to incorporate character education effectively into schools and classrooms and how to involve parents.

Over the years we have collected a number of questions from our conversations with teachers interested in character education. These are the questions we plan to answer in a clear and concise way in this book. These questions are at the core for educating the minds and hearts of children and young people. We have arranged these questions into four sections. Section I includes the frequently asked questions about character, values, and character education. We call these the foundational questions. Section II addresses the questions teachers ask about instruction. Section III answers questions about curriculum and materials, schoolwide activities, and how to work effectively with parents and community members. The last section provides readings and resources, programs and organizations.

This book sets the framework for a new K-5 character education program from Argus Education. The *Argus Character Education*

1

Program: Teaching Literacy and Character was developed on the basis of strong research in both character education and literacy development. The program effectively integrates the teaching of six character traits with the teaching of language arts/reading. Informed and driven by the daily realities and requirements of the teacher, the program gets up to speed very quickly supporting the reading curriculum and accelerating student knowledge of character. Note that, although this primer includes lessons and activities created by teachers and character education consultants, we, the authors, do not endorse those lessons and activities.

Professionals like yourself are very busy and have limited time to read volumes on any topic. This primer will give you the overview you need to better understand the character education movement that is taking place in classrooms, schools, and communities. It is our invitation to you to engage in the character education of children and youth. We make no pretense that this is the last word on the topic. Consider this primer to be your introduction. Using a question-and-answer format, we hope to entice you to investigate further this important reform movement to help children and youth learn and practice the positive personal values of being humane and human, the social values of behaving responsibly and ethically, and the application of values that are the glue in a democratic society.
Begin by reflecting on your answers to two crucial questions: If schools do not assist parents in the character development of their children, then to whom can parents turn? If we don't do it now, then when should we do it?

Foundational Questions

What Is Character?

*I have a dream that my four children will one day live in
a nation where they will not be judged by the color of their
skin, but by the content of their character.*[1]

Martin Luther King, Jr.

The word character comes from a Greek word meaning "stylus," an
instrument that is used "to engrave." Webster's[2] dictionary
defines character as "a distinctive trait, quality, or attribute; one's
moral constitution; the pattern of behavior or personality found in an
individual."

When we talk about character and character education, we will
use two words synonymously—values and traits. The personal trait
(a distinguished quality) of honesty, is also a civic value (a principle,
trait, or virtue accepted by our society). A person develops character
early in life through his or her experiences and relationships.
Experiences and relationships "engrave" on a person's personality
certain traits that guide that person's behavior and actions. The
Argus Character Education Program highlights six traits that have

3

emerged from a poll of educators and consultants: respect, responsibility, honesty, trustworthiness, effort, and kindness. These and other character traits and values will be identified as we discuss the answers to the questions presented in this book.

We might say, then, that each person has a personal character and a civic character. Personal character is an accumulation of traits that predispose one to do that which is right, to reflect on moral matters, to be a good and ethical person, a person who knows right from wrong, a person who acts in a manner consistent with the "Golden Rule," that is, treat others as you would want to be treated.

Civic character encompasses the personal traits and also includes such traits as respect for laws, responsibility, fairness, justice, and knowing and participating in public affairs. Voting, being of service to others, and volunteering are examples of a person applying civic character.

As you can see, character is learned. It is shaped by factors seen and unseen. It consists of a list of positive personal and civic traits (some call them virtues, others call them values) that vary. For example, one list suggests values for persons of good character using the letters of the word itself as follows:

C = caring
H = honesty
A = acceptance
R = respect
A = altruism
C = compassion
T = trustworthy
E = empathy
R = responsibility

The important point here, as stated in the Aspen Declaration on Character Education (1992), is that "the present and future well-being of our society requires an involved, caring citizenry with good moral character. . . . People do not automatically develop good moral character; therefore, conscientious efforts must be made to help young people develop the values (traits) and abilities necessary for moral decision and conduct."[3] Lickona reminds us that "good character consists of knowing the good, desiring the good, and doing the good—habits of the mind, habits of the heart, and habits of action."[4]

What Is Character Education?

> *Effective character education is based on core ethical values which form the foundation of democratic society, in particular, respect, responsibility, trustworthiness, caring, justice and fairness, civic virtue and citizenship.*[5]
> Aspen Declaration on Character Education, 1992

If character is learned, and if it involves one's experiences and relationships, then schools have a role to play. Schools are the one place where children and youth come together to learn, examine, and apply positive character traits. We call this character education.

There are many definitions of character education. Let's hear from those who have written in the field to give you a better sense of what character education means: Ryan claims that the popularity of the word character and character education results from its emphasis on the concepts of "socialization"[6]. Kirschenbaum points out that character education is now the preferable term for the teaching of traditional values and moral virtues[7]. According to Berreth and Berman, character education "is helping young people develop a sense of social responsibility. . .; helping students understand, through experiences, that what they value matters and that living these virtues (responsibility, respect, self-discipline, integrity, and empathy) lends meaning and richness to their own lives."[8]

London says that character education means two things: "1) education in civic virtue and in the qualities that teach children the forms and rules of citizenship in a just society; and 2) that enable children to become productive and dependable citizens."[9]

Here is our definition of character education.

Character education:

- Is a concerted effort by the community and the schools to educate children and youth about an agreed-upon set of values
- Begins in a family setting

- Occurs when children and youth witness and imitate adults and peers modeling the consensus values
- Occurs when students come to know the values through the school environment and its curriculum and co-curricular activities
- Occurs when students study, clarify, reflect, reason, decide, and act upon the consensus values
- Is enhanced when students are guided and supervised in applying the values at school and in the community
- Is verified when students and stakeholders assess and model the consensus values[10]

These definitions should help you understand character education. As you read these and other definitions, certain themes surface: character development, traits of character, specific civic values, consensus or core values, socialization and democratic principles, and civic learning and participation.

The definitions of character education help set what might be a "vision" of a comprehensive character education program. We see that vision to be:

- Schools as communities of learners where clear, consistent, coherent, and congruent messages are communicated to all about goals, expectations, learning, and behavior
- Schools where all students are learning the values, attitudes, skills, and knowledge that they will need to become successful and productive citizens in a democratic society
- School and community environments that nurture adherence to democratic principles, respectful relationships, civility, responsibility, trust, loyalty, collaboration, and care
- Schools with high expectations for students' academic achievement and for their personal, prosocial, and civic behavior.

This vision is what character education is all about. But one question remains: Why do we need to address the character development of the young? Both personal and cultural events over the last three decades clearly suggest that there is an important need to be concerned about the character development of the young as we enter the 21st century.

Why Is Character Education Needed?

The impetus for character education is drawn from the observation that there is a crisis in society because of the culture's inability to transmit a set of core values and virtues to youth.[11]

J. Leming, "Character Education
and Clinical Intervention," 1997

You have read the headlines and the stories behind the headlines about the young killing the young; about bullying, harassing, hazing, incivility, and foul language; about cheating, lying, and stealing. You have read about the disintegration of the family unit, about the concern for safety in our schools and streets, and about the erosion of ethics, virtues, and character. Books and articles have been written about the isolation of the young from the adult world and about a self-centered culture where the demand for rights outstrips the need for responsibility.

One important reason for character education efforts in schools and communities is to address these disturbing trends by teaching and encouraging young people to learn and practice moral reasoning, emotional control, prosocial behaviors, and positive personal and civic values.

A second reason for the need for character education addresses the question, "If we (educators and parents) don't do it, who will?" The answer is technology, peers, the media, and the marketplace. Is this where our young should be learning their values and behaviors? We, like you, don't think so.

Third, many state education codes, laws, and mandates have identified character education as an educational priority. To support state efforts, the U.S. Department of Education has awarded character education pilot project grants to more than 30 states over the past five years. In the year 2000, for example, 9 states received million-dollar grants. In addition, in communities throughout the country, businesses and organizations have recognized the importance of the school's initiatives in this area and have sponsored many school and community events related to character education.

A fourth reason centers around the changing nature of the young people attending schools. In 1994, superintendents of schools across the United States were surveyed about the changes they observed among the students in their schools over the years. Their list addresses such concerns as dysfunctional families, technology, changing communities, crime and violence, ignorance and poverty, mass media, questioning of authority, shunning traditional values and responsibilities, a lack of a sense of community, and peer influences on values.[12]

Fifth, our conversations with teachers and administrators reveal a concern for such student behaviors as rudeness; uncivil, inappropriate language; irresponsibility; disrespect; willingness to blame others; inability to distinguish right from wrong; impulsiveness and impatience; and inattentiveness and aggressiveness. To be sure, there are many students, as our colleagues are quick to point out, who have learned and model the positive character traits that we talk about in this book. However, there is a growing number of students whose behavior at school disrupts class instruction and the culture of the school.

The "why" question can be summarized as follows:

Character: demonstrating moral reasoning, critical thinking, the Golden Rule, values/traits, ethical behavior, and self-control

Career: having cognitive and social skills, personal traits, decision-making skills, and problem-solving skills; knowing how to learn; and participating in teamwork and collaboration

Citizenship: having civic knowledge and understandings (social justice); participating; contributing; voting; volunteering (service); and valuing the benefits of living in a democratic, multicultural society

In making their case for character education, Ryan and Bohlin offer five "arguments" that favor character education in our schools. The first they call "the argument from intellectual authorities" from Plato to Dewey, from Kant to Confucius. Second, our founding fathers made a strong case in favor of character education. Their third argument focuses on state laws. Fourth is public opinion. Polls have told us for years that the public wants schools to teach values, democracy, tolerance, patriotism, moral courage, and the Golden Rule. The fifth argument suggested by the authors is what they call the "inevitability argument". That is, it is unlikely that students can go through 12 or so years of schooling without their character and values being affected by their school experiences.[13]

How Can We Implement Character Education Initiatives in Our School and Community?

The development of character requires the rigorous train-
ing of the whole being in the same way as athletic or musi-
cal development requires extensive training. The power to
make good choices and develop good character is aided by
this training.[14]

P. Glanzer, "The Character
to Seek Justice," 1998

Our work in character education over the past decade has led us to conclude that for schools to implement effective character education initiatives, a comprehensive framework must be in place. Our intent here is to offer you an overview of the components of a framework we have developed over the years. We strongly suggest that you and your colleagues read our work on this topic for a more comprehensive discussion of the framework and each of its components.[15] In this summary, our focus will be the school site and its character education stakeholders (supporters of the school's character education initiatives).

Leadership

In most, if not all schools, the leadership of the school rests with the school principal. The support of the principal for the school's character education initiatives is essential, but equally important is the need to share that leadership with others. Leadership shared is leadership earned. Thus, each school should create a Character Education Council (CEC) with members representing administrators, teachers, parents, classified personnel, community leaders, and, where appropriate, students. The purpose of the council is to take a leadership role in assuring that each of the components of the framework is implemented.

Expectations

By expectations we mean the mission, the goals, the consensus on values, and the anticipated outcomes of a school's character education efforts. Expectations offer possible answers to the "Why" and "What" questions: Why do you want a character education program? Why is such a program important to the school, the students, and the community? What is your mission, your intent, your goals? What outcomes will you be looking for? What consensus values will underscore all the school initiatives?

Here is an example. In our meetings in a middle school regarding its character education interests, the school's personnel decided that the consensus values for the school would be responsibility, compassion, respect, the Golden Rule, honesty, self-discipline, cooperation, perseverance, and tolerance. Their mission was to create a safe, nurturing, and challenging school environment that infused these core values into all aspects of school life. Their expectations of the outcomes of the program were that students would:

- Demonstrate an understanding of multiple perspectives,
- Exhibit positive attitudes toward learning and school,
- Demonstrate responsibility for their own learning,
- Demonstrate a concern for the welfare of others,
- Respect adults and each other more often,
- Apply ethical decision-making skills to solving problems, and
- Demonstrate skills of social cooperation.

Climate

Character education programs have little hope of being successful when housed in a school where the environment is negative, distracting, competitive, discouraging, nonsupportive, or distrustful. Research on the elements of a positive school climate suggest that these factors must be in place: high academic and behavioral expectations, strong collaborative leadership, an orderly environment, coherence of policies and procedures, effective communication, and high student and teacher morale. In our book for school administrators, we provide a list of 50 ways to improve the climate of a school and pose 40 questions for assessing a school's climate.[16] Research and common sense suggest that character education efforts will not only help change the climate of a school and each classroom, but these initiatives must take place in an environment that welcomes the implementation of the consensus values and lets these values permeate the culture of the school.

Implementation

There are specific criteria to which character education stakeholders should attend when implementing character education initiatives at the school site. We have called these the *Implementation Criteria* (the 11 Cs): courage, commitment, collaboration, communication, caring, consensus, change, culture, connections, coherence, and critical.[17] These 11 criteria are interrelated and should be integrated in all school site character education initiatives. We have grouped the 11 Cs and provided a short explanation of each to give you an overview of the criteria for implementing a comprehensive, long-lasting, and effective character education program.

Courage and Commitment. Teachers, administrators, and some parents tell us that it takes courage and commitment to implement character education initiatives in a school. It takes courage and commitment to keep stakeholders informed about the need for the character development of children to take place in school. It takes courage and commitment to assume a leadership role, to be out front leading efforts to implement a character education program. It takes courage and commitment to educate the reluctant, to challenge the fence dwellers, and to manage the go-getters. It takes courage and commitment to form coalitions, to organize stakeholders, and to implement these criteria and the standards discussed elsewhere in this book. It takes courage and commitment to address the concerns about where to put character education in an already full school day with limited teacher time. It takes courage and commitment to answer the question: "Will this program help us increase the test scores of children in this school?" And it takes courage and commitment to be held accountable for one's views and actions and the program's results.

Collaboration and Communication. Collaboration is more than cooperation. It is a commitment by people to spend time and energy over an extended period of time to implement the school's character education initiatives. Communication enhances collaboration; collaboration underscores each of the 11 Cs. Collaboration and communication start with the school's Character Education Council (CEC). It is CEC members who ensure that school personnel, parents, students, and the community support the program's consensus/core values and its programs and activities. It is the CEC who utilize effective communication techniques to keep stakeholders informed and involved. It is the CEC who implements this framework and each of the 11 Cs.

Caring and Consensus. The one value that underpins all character education initiatives is caring. The consensus among all stakeholders involved in character education work is that they care for the character development of children, that they care for the relationships that take place between adults and the young, and that they care about the environment of the school, home, and neighborhood.

If consensus cannot be reached on the value of caring, then it is unlikely that other values will be agreed upon by stakeholders. Values such as respect, responsibility, honesty, trustworthiness, empathy, and the like, have their roots in the value of care.

In this regard, we agree with Noddings, who believes that the themes of care should permeate the school culture and the instructional program. She says that "we can use the rich vocabulary of care in educational planning and introduce themes of care into the regular subject matter classes."[18]

Change and Culture. Implementing character education requires a school culture open to change. It requires a culture that will enable stakeholders to learn, to study, to cope with ambiguity, to deal with uncertainty, to engage in new experiences, to try new ways of doing things, and to assess what is being done and how it is working.

Character education is all about change. Change is all about trying to do something differently for the benefit of all involved. This requires a school culture that is inviting rather than restrictive, collaborative rather than divisive, and inclusive rather than exclusive.

A positive school culture/climate is essential to change and to the implementation of character education initiatives. There are many examples of negative school cultures being changed by a new school principal who rallies stakeholders to make the school a better place to teach and learn. In these cases, the principal, with the help of other school leaders, implemented new programs and policies and developed better procedures and practices. Through effective communication and collaboration, the implementation of character education initiatives, in some cases, changed the culture of the school.

Connections and Coherence. Just as all things in life are connected, so it is with character education. We look to the components of this character education framework as the coherent and connecting factors for a school's character education efforts. As you examine each component of the framework, it is obvious that none can stand alone. For example, the goals component is connected to the outcomes component; training is connected to the resource component; and assessment is connected to all of the components. Coherence (unity, connection, adhesion) is the glue of the framework and is essential when implementing, maintaining, and evaluating a school's character education initiatives.

We believe deeply that students need to see a connection and coherence among the subjects they are taught and the values they learn. They need to see a connection between personal values and civic values. They need to see and practice the connections between the Golden Rule and service. As Gene Maeroff describes it:

> Connectedness operates in several ways to equip young people with the social capital that helps them negotiate their success. On one level, connectedness means gaining a feeling of belonging so that students regard themselves as part of the academic enterprise. On another level, it means developing ties that they can use to thread their way around obstacles. The sense of connectedness is strengthened by bonds that the school establishes with home,

neighborhood, and community.[19]

Critical. We use this word to mean that all character education stakeholders at a school must make informed judgments about their character education work and outcomes; there is a critical need for assessment and accountability. We will discuss this topic at greater length when we address the assessment component of the framework (see page 17).

Standards

A standard is a measure of quantity, quality, or value established by general consent.[20] We use the word standards in this book to mean "quality—the ideal or good" for which participants strive. Standards set the bar for achievement, performance, and behavior. Standards are becoming the *modus operandi* of our work in schools and, in general, the standards movement has public support.

Recently, The Public Agenda, a non-profit, nonpartisan public policy research organization, released a report titled *Survey Finds Little Sign of Backlash Against Academic Standards or Standardized Tests.*[21] As the title implies, a majority of parents support the establishment of standards and achievement testing. We, too, joined the standards movement by creating character education standards that apply to teaching, programs, curriculum, partnerships, and assessment.[22] We did so for two reasons. One, we found standards absent from the character education literature. Two, we thought it best to provide educators like yourself with principles that would guide practice—principles against which one could evaluate certain aspects of their character education initiatives.

Training

Section II of this book discusses specific instructional strategies that are useful for teaching students about character and the school's consensus values. However, it is wise to use caution when implementing character education initiatives without sufficient preparation for the stakeholders who will be expected to participate fully in the school's character education programs and activities.

- Parents need help understanding what it means to be a

child's first moral educator.

- Teachers need to understand why they are character educators and to engage in discussions about child development.
- Teachers and parents need to know and understand the importance of modeling.
- Teachers need to know which instructional strategies will help them carry out the tenets of the school's character education program.
- Administrators need to know why and how to take leadership roles in their school's character education efforts.
- Counselors need to understand their responsibilities in the school's efforts to teach children good character.
- All school personnel need ongoing discussions about their roles as models for promoting and practicing the school's core values.
- Students need to be engaged in all character education efforts at the school, take leadership roles, and participate fully in programs and activities.

For these reasons, all parties affected by a school's character education program will benefit from training. It is about educating all stakeholders about child and character development, about values and character traits, about mentoring and modeling, about citizenship and service, and about program implementation, strategies, maintenance, and assessment.

Partnerships

Partnerships are critical to a school's character education efforts because it takes families, agencies, and whole communities to raise a child with good character. Schools cannot and should not attempt to engage in the character development of children and youth without involving parents and others. Parents cannot do it without the help of family, friends, and the institutions that serve them and their children.

It is a good idea for the CEC at each school to take on the responsibilities of forming partnerships. In schools that are large enough, personnel can create a partnership action team. We have developed seven partnership standards:

- The school's character education efforts must be in close concert with parents. Forming effective partnerships is essential to the success of any character education program.
- Parents, guardians, and child care providers should be active participants in character education program planning and evaluation.
- The character education program will provide homes with full-service opportunities to help meet the physical, social, and emotional needs of children.
- All school personnel need skills to assist parents in helping children become successful learners and to help parents cope with problems of raising children.
- School personnel in middle and high schools must make special efforts to maintain parental involvement with the schools to help foster character education.
- Community agencies and businesses can do a great deal to help parents become involved in the cognitive and moral development of their children.
- School personnel must "care" about parental involvement; they must "communicate" frequently and effectively with parents; they must value "collaboration"; they must have a "coherent" plan of action; and they must be willing to "change" the factors that detract from the creation of effective home, school, and community partnerships.[23]

In addition to our seven partnership standards, the National Parent Teacher Association recommends seven standards that support parent involvement programs. Their seven standards address communication, parenting, student learning, volunteering, advocacy, decision making, and community collaboration.[24] These standards state the obvious, but what is obvious is sometimes overlooked. Strong, effective character education partnerships between the school and families, and between the school and the community, must address the issues of relationships, involvement, communication, feedback, advocacy, problem solving, and decision making.

Resources

16

The recommendation here is easy (to say, but not to do) and straightforward: to implement a character education initiative, school personnel and character education stakeholders need time and money: money to buy time and secure resources; time to prepare, to learn, to investigate, and to plan; time to train teachers, engage and involve parents, and network with community leaders; time and resources to attend conferences and workshops, to visit schools, to plan programs and activities, to purchase materials and support students activities; and time and resources to decide what and how to evaluate processes, procedures, and outcomes.

Assessment

The last component of the framework is no less important than the other components. You and the stakeholders at your school need to know the results of your efforts to develop children's character. The only way to do this is to appreciate the value in evaluation and then seek answers to questions about the program and anticipated outcomes.

We believe in action research and collaborative evaluation where stakeholders at the school site work cooperatively to find out the effects of their character education efforts. To do this, stakeholders need to follow these guidelines:

- Organize for evaluation purposes. Either the tasks are done by the CEC or another committee of the council.
- Take time to discuss the purposes of evaluation. Think about why it should be done and investigate what others do to evaluate their character education programs.
- Use the W and H questions to help in planning for evaluation. What should be evaluated? Why should it be evaluated? When should it be evaluated? Who will **do it?** How will it be done? What resources will be **needed?** How will the data be collected?
- Don't try to evaluate too much too soon. Set a timetable to evaluate in two-year cycles, and as a general rule plan on assessing two or three items per year.
- Focus on the goals and anticipated outcomes.

17

- Have evaluation plans accompany program development plans. In other words, evaluate as you implement programs and procedures.
- Once the data is collected, decide how it will be collated, analyzed, and reported.
- Take time to study and discuss what the findings mean for changing, modifying, or dropping current practices. Let the findings "drive" action plans.

In summary, the "how to" question was answered by outlining the components of a comprehensive character education framework for schools. We note the importance of leadership, the need to identify programmatic and behavioral expectations, and the importance of an acceptable, caring school climate. These three components set the school environment for character education. Once a receptive environment has been established, we recommend that you address implementation standards. To do this, we described how to use the 11 criteria (11 Cs), such as courage, commitment, and collaboration. Now, it is time to address the concern about the impact of the school's character education initiatives.

Does Character Education Pay Off?

Correct principles are like compasses; they are always pointing the way. And if we know how to read them, we won't get lost, confused, or fooled by conflicting voices and values.[25]

S. Covey
Principle-Centered Leadership, 1991

Covey poses a fair and important question because it addresses both accountability and the need to know if certain practices are better than others. A few examples paint the "pay off" picture.

Leming studied character education programs and found that those that report "encouraging results" are those that have a positive social climate, clear standards, mutual respect between teachers and students, shared governance, effective communication, support by stakeholders, student involvement, clear, fair and enforceable rules, orderly schools and classrooms, and the use of cooperative learning strategies.[26]

The Child Development Project, an elementary school character education program endorsed by the National Association of Elementary School Principals and one of the most well-researched programs, reports that if students feel a "sense of classroom community" they have more academic motivation and better performance, greater liking for school, greater empathy for others, more frequent altruistic behavior, better skills in resolving conflicts, and a higher sense of efficacy.[27]

Lakeside Middle School's (Atlanta, Georgia) commitment to character education focused on discipline problems and student test scores. Using "character commitment words of the week" (38 words) which were infused into the curriculum and schoolwide activities, involving parents, and using incentives offered by the business community, their disciplinary problems decreased and test scores improved significantly.[28]

Character education programs are reporting positive results regarding the school climate, student attendance, discipline referrals, teacher morale, parent involvement, classroom environment, student behavior and attitudes, and, in some cases, better academic achievement. You can't go wrong. The next three sections of this book describe teaching strategies, curriculum, and program and partnership ideas, along with available resources for you to use to begin this important work.

> *The schools should have given them [students] some sort of intellectual and moral key to their contemporary world.*[29]
>
> J. Dewey,
> Problems of Men, 1946

SECTION
II

Instructional Questions

Which Teaching Strategies Are Recommended?

Train up a child in the way he should go: and when he is old, he will not depart from it.[30]

Proverbs, 22:6

Teaching makes the difference with character education. In addition to having the best programs, materials, motivational speakers, or committee meetings at a school site, character educators must also be caring and enthusiastic and have knowledge about the strategies and skills necessary to reach the program's objectives. In short, in order to be an effective character educator, you need access to resources and training.

Some teaching strategies are more effective than others when teaching the school's core values. The teaching strategies described in this section have been gathered over years of working with teachers in schools and in workshops, academies, and seminars. We call it the "Teaching Framework," or 8 Cs. If used regularly, this set of strategies can be effective in helping children and youth reach character education objectives. The 8 Cs are:

- Connections: teacher modeling

- Constructivism: a student-centered approach
- Classroom Climate: creating a community of learners
- Classroom Management: intrinsic motivation, rules, and rewards
- Critical Thinking: ethical decision making, higher-order thinking, and questioning
- Conflict Resolution: mediation and problem-solving strategies
- Cooperative Learning: the significance of interdependence
- Community Service Learning: citizenship and democratic practices

These 8 Cs are the guides for how a teacher implements character education and describes his/her role and responsibilities in the classroom. As the teacher, you need to be prepared to adapt these strategies to match up with your curricular goals and standards, whatever the content area and grade level might be. Many of these strategies are familiar ones, and books and articles have been written on the importance of each one. Most, if not all, character education experts agree on the importance of the 8 Cs. Below, we describe each of these teaching strategies and then include examples and some tips about how to use these strategies to reach character education objectives.

Connections

> *The most persuasive moral teaching we adults do is by example: the witness of our lives, our ways of being with others and speaking to them and getting on with them— all of that is taken in slowly, cumulatively, by . . . our students*[31].

R. Coles, The Moral
Intelligence of Children, 1997

As Coles alludes, making connections deals with relationships. Relationships between students and teachers, students and students, and teachers and staff. One of Maslow's basic human needs is for "a sense of belonging." Without positive connections to others, students will seek connections that may be negative (such as joining a gang).

On a basic level, students need to make connections to their peers and with staff. This is often accomplished in cooperative groups and by individual staff members one-on-one with students but is more often reached in advisory groups or on teams. Relationships extend to the content of the curriculum. Students need to make connections with the content and learn about the connectedness between subjects. That happens most often when students are engaged in lessons. On a larger level, students need to make connections to school and to the community. This connection is often made through schoolwide or co-curricular activities, such as sports, drama, the debate club, or community service learning projects.

A teacher makes the most significant connections with students through modeling. As Williams wrote, "The most effective teachers are the ones who model the values they want their students to learn."[32] Research indicates that students pay more attention to what a teacher does than to what he or she says.[33] There are certain qualities (attributes) that are found in teachers that students perceive to be those of a model character educator. Some of these attributes are helping, explaining, questioning, showing respect, being tolerant, being encouraging, providing guidance, being nice, polite, liking to help students, being success-oriented (believing in students' capabilities), and being involved (modeling, trusting, truthful).[34]

Another important aspect of modeling is that students learn values from a teacher, whether the teacher is aware of it or not. Modeling has a powerful influence on student behavior, both positive and negative, so teachers need to practice what they preach. In fact, if you, the teacher, don't model the values you ask students to follow, the students may not learn the core values promoted by the school.

Following are six teaching tips for helping your students make connections:

1. Build relationships with students, with parents, and between students.
2. Listen to students and include their ideas (when possible) in lessons.
3. Be a model of the behavior you expect from students.

4. Encourage students to participate in setting classroom rules and rewards.
5. Create a climate in the classroom that is safe and nurturing.
6. Make time in your lessons for activities that help students apply the core values.

Note the key words we have used to describe what we mean by connections. Each word is a powerful reminder to teachers about how to connect with their students. Three key words—caring, relationships, and modeling—should inform your interactions with the students in your classroom and the way you instruct them.

Constructivism

> *We honor our children by taking the moral and spiritual side of their lives seriously and by thinking how we might respond to it with tact and intelligence.*[35]
>
> R. Coles, The Moral
> Intelligence of Children, 1997

Constructivism is based on the premise that through individual experiences we construct our own perspectives of the world. Some basic components of constructivism are that each person constructs knowledge from experience, that learning is a personal interpretation, that learning is an active process of making meaning related to experiences, that people share multiple perspectives, and that people can change their thinking through collaborative learning.[36] Constructivists believe that learning should take place in real-life settings, and testing should be integrated with assignments and not be a separate activity.

The question uppermost on a constructivist teacher's mind is "What is the right thing to do for each child?" We believe this is also the ethical thing to do. The following teaching tips will help you to be both a constructivist and a character educator.

- Encourage and accept student autonomy.
- Use concrete materials and primary sources.
- Use higher-level cognitive terms (classify, predict, and evaluate).
- Allow student responses to drive lessons.

- Adjust content and teaching strategies to respond to students' needs.
- Inquire about students' understanding.
- Encourage students to engage in dialogue.
- Encourage student inquiry by asking good questions and encouraging students to ask questions.
- Ask students to elaborate on their responses.
- Create a sense of mutual trust and respect in the classroom.
- Provide time for students to construct relationships and apply ideas.[37]

If you want to be a character educator, constructivism means putting your students first. You need to find a way to connect constructivist principles to your classroom teaching practices.

Classroom Climate

> *A community, a supportive and challenging social environment, is essential for children's intellectual, social, and ethical development.*[38]

J. Dalton and M. Watson,
Among Friends, 1997

Classroom climate refers to both the physical environment and ethos (sense of community). Creating a sense of community in the classroom, when you have more than 30 students in a class, is not easy. Students need to get to know each other, trust each other, work together, value each other, and feel safe. Dalton and Watson would assert that the classroom environment needs to be nurturing, caring, and challenging.

The reason for creating a positive climate is that the classroom environment will foster a sense of community that will help students learn the school's core values. A classroom with a positive climate is one that is caring, civil, and democratic; has high expectations for both academics and behavior; and is a place where each of these 8 Cs are implemented. Research confirms that "the factors that are most significant in school efforts to foster character include the school atmosphere (not the formal school curricula and traditional approaches), the personal characteristics of teachers, the teacher's role, teacher-student relationships, and the classroom climate."[39]

Use these teacher tips to build a sense of community in your classroom:

- Create a community of learners by using activities, such as cooperative learning, role plays, debates, and simulations.
- Use conflict resolution strategies to help students learn to take responsibility for their own actions and solve their own problems peacefully.
- Incorporate community service learning into your lessons so students can put their knowledge and beliefs into action, while making connections to the larger community.
- Hold class meetings to connect students to each other and to the content and process of the classroom, and provide your students experiences with democratic principles.

We urge you to consider class meetings as part of your instructional repertoire. We agree with our colleague Lickona, who says that "A class meeting . . . is the single most important support system for eliciting and strengthening students' best values and behavior."[40] Class meetings help to create a sense of community in the classroom that contributes to a positive classroom climate.

Classroom Management

> *Do not count on extrinsic rewards to cultivate virtues . . .*
> *virtuous behavior needn't always be rewarded. Character*
> *education is about inspiring students to do the good;*
> *interesting them in worthwhile pursuits, both academic*
> *and extracurricular; and helping them to internalize good*
> *habits.*[41]

K. Ryan and K. Bohlin,
Building Character in Schools, 1999

You can try to control children with extrinsic motivators, such as stars and stickers, but it is more advantageous when you help children learn how to control themselves by linking classroom activities and lessons to a child's intrinsic motivation to learn and to belong. You can take advantage of these basic human drives in order to help children learn what they need to learn and cooperate with others in the classroom. This is the secret for effective classroom management.

Even if you have established a positive classroom climate and use constructivist teaching principles, behavior problems will arise. Each time a child misbehaves it becomes a teachable moment for character education. Your response to the child, combined with the child's degree of ownership of the classroom rules, facilitates that child's acceptance of the consequences and punishment. We highly recommend that you establish classroom rules and consequences with students in advance, allowing student voices and choices early on at the beginning of the school year. If a student has an opportunity to collaborate on rule setting, you will be much more likely to gain his or her cooperation in dealing with the consequences of misbehavior.

Basically, your goal should be to establish an environment in the classroom that makes being good or doing the right thing desirable for the students. As Watson reminds us, "Children subjected extensively to discipline based or external controls develop low internal commitment to good behavior."[42] Instead, Leming's findings are that character develops within the social climate. The nature of the environment, the messages it sends to individuals, and the behaviors it encourages and discourages are the important factors for character education. Clear rules of conduct, student ownership of the rules, a supportive environment, and satisfaction resulting from complying with the norms of the environment shape behavior.[43]

Here are some teaching tips we created from Kirshenbaum's guidelines for administering consequences and punishments:[44]

- Let the punishment fit the crime. Avoid harsh punishments for minor infractions, and avoid light reproofs for serious infractions. For example, if students deface school property, an appropriate punishment, rather than suspension, would be to require them to clean up the school grounds.
- Avoid mass punishment for individual infractions. Classroom-wide punishments for the actions of one or two students create feelings of resentment toward authority in a number of students who may feel unfairly punished.

- Be consistent, yet flexible. If a rule is applied inconsistently, children may become confused about its importance and resentful. However, it can be self-defeating to be too rigid. There may be a good reason to make an exception. There are times when a child's welfare is better served by setting aside a rule.
- Never use ridicule for negative feedback and punishment. Instead, let a child save face in front of his or her peers. When using criticism or punishment, always try to convey the idea that it is a child's particular behavior or choice which is inappropriate, and he or she must face the consequence for what he or she did. However, let the child know that you care about them as a person.

There are no easy answers to the question of how best to manage your classroom. Management factors include teaching style, needs of students, physical environment, support from parents and school administrators. There are no quick solutions to developing a democratic, caring, accepting classroom. It takes an investment of time. However, the returns, or the effect of the time spent on community building, enhances every interaction.[45]

Critical Thinking

> *Students need to practice reflection and rational inquiry throughout their experience with the curriculum. They need to be stretched discursively, dialoguing with their peers, their teachers, their readings, and themselves about moral themes and questions.*[46]

K. Ryan and K. Bohlin,
Building Character in Schools, 1999

Character educators help students learn how to think critically. Critical thinking encompasses a broad range of activities, including ethical decision making, higher-order thinking, and questioning. Thinking critically is related to the kinds of questions one asks. Closed-ended questions elicit responses about information (facts, commitments, declarations). Open-ended questions (the how, what, and why questions) usually encourage analysis, synthesis, and creativity in thinking. Writing orders, focuses, and stimulates thinking. Question asking, brainstorming, list making, model building, and application are all thinking skill strategies.

Let's take a classroom example of a fourth-grade teacher who wants to teach a beginning lesson on managing anger using questioning techniques to stimulate student thinking about this emotion. He or she might prepare the students for the lesson by having them read a story, read a news item, or watch a video clip of a person or people expressing anger and its results. He or she might show the students a variety of pictures of peoples' faces expressing a range of emotions and ask the students to sort out the pictures according to the emotion expressed—anger, happiness, joy, concern, or sadness (analysis, categorizing).

The teacher might then engage the students in a discussion of what they read or watched. Thus, some groundwork has been laid about the idea of emotions, particularly the emotion of anger, and how these are expressed. Next, the teacher could ask students to complete the following sentence: "When I get angry, I usually ____" or, "When I see a person get angry, he or she usually ____"

This prompt initiates the lesson. The answer to the question prompts responses. The teacher might use some or all of the following questions to continue the lesson on exploring ways to control anger: What is anger? Is getting mad bad? What happens to you physically when you get angry? How do you know that you are angry? Is it good to get angry? How does anger help? How is it not helpful?

The teacher might also include a story from the students' readers to which such questions are applicable. The students can discuss the answers to the questions for the character(s) in the book as well as reflect on their own answers to the questions. Video scenes of people getting mad might be used for analysis and discussion.

At this point in the lesson, the teacher might group the students, give each group a piece of newsprint and a pen, and ask them to develop a list of ideas that address the question, "What are some healthy ways a person can control anger?" (brainstorming). The teacher can then have students review group responses (analysis and evaluation) and decide on a list to be used by all students in the class (synthesis). Once posted, the teacher suggests that the students consider the items on the list when they are in situations that might cause anger. In a week or two, students could record in their journals whether or not they used any items on the list in situations that caused them to be angry (application). Prompt questions could be "What was the event that got you mad? Did you know you were angry? How did you know? Did our lesson come to your mind when you got mad? Did you think about anything on the list? Did you use any item on the list to help you control your anger? Did it work? Why? If it didn't work, why do you think that it didn't?"

Following are five teaching tips for fostering critical thinking in the classroom:

1. Your students' thinking skills develop, in part, from the quality of the questions you ask them. Questions stimulate thinking and learning. They are the brain's tool kit. So attend to the questions that you ask, particularly questions that require your students to analyze, synthesize, and evaluate information, ideas, and issues. Also, encourage your students to ask questions.

2. One writer says that "thinking is inner speech." Reading, writing, and discussing are three major ways for students to tap their thinking. Use journal writing, discussion groups, and reading material to help your students think through values, ethical dilemmas, and issues about which they are reading and talking.

3. Use newspaper and magazine items and articles to read about what people do and why they do it. For example, a recent news item told about a middle school boy who brought a gun to school and said he may have used it. Four of his friends said they knew he was going to do this but told no one. Have your students talk about the "why" question and the values of loyalty vs. responsibility.

4. Before starting a lesson ask your students to think about the purposes of the lesson, what they know, what they would like to know, what procedures they need to follow to find answers, what steps they need to take to complete the lesson, what timelines need to be followed, and what their responsibilities are.

5. Here are six questions to use when asking students to think about their behavior or when two or more students get into a conflict. Have them take a time-out and write their answers to these questions: "What happened? When did it happen? Where did it happen? Who was involved? How did it happen? Why did it happen?"

Conflict Resolution

The moral life of the classroom is full of opportunities to teach children to handle conflict constructively.[47]

T. Lickona,
Educating for Character, 1991

Conflict is all around us and cannot be avoided, yet most of us are uncomfortable with it. Conflict resolution skills are usually taught in a schoolwide peer mediation program. Lickona's quote reminds us that a teacher does not need to have a schoolwide program in place to integrate conflict resolution skills into the classroom. Two of the best vehicles for this at the classroom level are class meetings and role plays. Role playing solutions to conflict situations makes it more likely that students will actually apply the conflict resolution skills when they need them. An important outcome related to character education is that it teaches students self-control and responsibility for resolving their own conflicts.

Most children lack the skills necessary to deal with conflict constructively. These skills include communication skills (listening and verbal/nonverbal messages), problem-solving skills (identifying problems, brainstorming solutions, finding win-win solutions), and cooperative skills (working collaboratively to complete tasks). These conflict resolution skills should be taught to students through situations that allow them to practice using the skills in realistic contexts. Students need frequent guided practice in these skills to make them feel comfortable enough to use them to resolve conflicts when they arise.

Teaching students conflict resolution skills helps schools and classrooms become more conducive to student learning. Programs that use external rewards and punishments teach students that others in authority are needed to resolve conflicts. Students do not learn the skills and attitudes required to solve conflicts peacefully. Programs using intrinsic awards teach students how to behave in socially acceptable ways. Students learn how to monitor their own behavior, assess situations, and consider other people's perspectives, before acting.[48] The programs that use intrinsic rewards are the most successful in the long term. While students learn self-control and how to regulate their own behavior, they also learn positive personal values, prosocial behaviors, and citizenship skills. The benefits of conflict resolution look similar to those for cooperative learning and, according to Enright, add "higher levels of interpersonal understanding and an ability to reason about fairness."[49]

Lickona offers some tips for teaching conflict resolution skills in the classroom:

- Structure skill training to coach students in conflict avoidance and conflict resolution skills.
- Use class meetings to address common conflicts that occur among class members and to establish the norm of solving conflicts fairly and nonviolently.
- Intervene when necessary to help children apply their interpersonal skills at the moment of an actual conflict.
- Make students increasingly responsible for working out their own conflicts without the aid of an adult.[50]

There have been numerous articles published on how best to resolve conflicts in schools and classrooms. There are several specific conflict resolution programs and many teacher training opportunities. But, the bottom line, as we have suggested above, is the need to build positive relationships in your classroom, help students think critically about their behavior, make instruction interesting and stimulating, and let your students help you focus on problem-solving behaviors rather than punishing strategies.

Cooperative Learning

Using cooperative learning a majority of the time in the

*classroom creates positive relationships among students
and improves their level of achievement and psychological
well-being. Such an environment also affects teachers'
attitudes and competencies.*[51]

Johnson and Johnson,
Reducing School Violence, 1995

Just putting students in groups does not guarantee that they will work cooperatively to complete a task. You create a cooperative context by structuring a majority of learning situations cooperatively and applying the five essential elements of cooperation, based on the work of Johnson and Johnson:

1. The first element is positive interdependence, a tenet which holds that one student cannot succeed unless everyone succeeds. The following methods can help you structure positive interdependence in a group: group goals, joint rewards, divided resources, and complementary roles.

2. The second element is individual accountability. This means that you must assess each student's performance. You can structure individual accountability by testing each student individually or randomly selecting one student's product to represent the group.

3. The third element is face-to-face promotive interaction, or maximizing the opportunity for students to promote each other's efforts to learn. This is most successful in small groups of up to four students. You can facilitate this by asking students to help their group mates by explaining how to solve a problem, discuss a concept, or share ideas.

4. The fourth element is social skills, which are interpersonal and small group skills. Social skills include decision making, trust building, communication, and conflict management.

5. The fifth element is group processing, in which members discuss how well they are achieving goals and maintaining effective working relationships. Some keys to successful group processing are allowing sufficient time, making goals specific, and reminding students to use social skills.[52]

The research conducted on the effects of cooperative learning on student behavior identified several positive student outcomes. We recommend that you find a way to integrate cooperative learning into your lessons. Here is a list of student outcomes that you could match up with your content and character-building objectives:

- Student achievement is higher.
- Students gain greater competencies in critical thinking, attitude toward subjects, and working collaboratively.
- Students perceive grading as "fair."
- Students maintain positive relationships by demonstrating an acceptance of diverse students.
- Students have higher levels of self-esteem.
- Students exhibit greater cognitive and effective perspective-taking.[53]

All character educators agree in the power of cooperative learning as part of the instructional process in character education, because it combines the teaching of values and academics.[54]

Community Service Learning

> *How to address the matter of how we teachers might encourage our students (encourage ourselves) to take that big step from thought to action, from moral analysis to fulfilled moral commitments? Community service offers us all a chance to put our money where our mouths are.*[55]
> D. W. Johnson and R. T. Johnson,
> Reducing School Violence
> Through Conflict Resolution, 1995

We might say that service is one way of demonstrating citizenship. No doubt your school has or is considering community service learning programs. Our focus here is at the classroom level where you have the opportunity to help your students be good citizens through service.

We emphasize once again that both service and citizenship require one to be informed, involved, and introspective. Service, like charity, begins at home. Parents know this but they need your help.

It makes no sense to plan service projects for your classroom or community without working with parents to plan projects in the home. Both complement the virtues of service—the Golden Rule, caring, compassion, empathy, acceptance, respect, and responsibility.

In your classroom, just think of the number of service projects you might encourage students to do: tutoring each other, tutoring children in other grades, reading books to younger children, completing daily management tasks in class, having the students assume responsibility for playground safety and cleanliness, conducting a class food drive, starting a buddy system for new students, and instituting peer mediation teams. The class can brainstorm ways in which they can be of service in the home, in the community, and in their own classroom and school. The class can select one project they wish to do and then create a plan. Over time, students can create plans for each category—home, classroom, school, community. Students can do reports, keep journals, and hold discussions about their service learning experiences.

Teachers, like yourself, are teaching citizenship and democratic principles through service projects with excitement and fervor. You "no longer see it as an add-on activity but as an innovative strategy for teaching content standards, raising academic achievement, and empowering young people to become civic-minded and committed to addressing the needs of their community."[56]

Our teaching tips that follow summarize Wiley's Principles of Good Practice for Combining Service and Learning.[57] Combining service and learning:

- Engages people in responsible and challenging actions for the common good
- Is committed to program participation by and with diverse populations
- Allows for those with needs to define those needs
- Matches service providers and service needs
- Expects genuine, active, and sustained organizational commitment
- Includes training, supervision, monitoring, support, recognition, and evaluation to meet goals
- Ensures that the time commitment is flexible, appropriate,

and in the best interests of all involved

- Provides structured opportunities for people to reflect critically on their experience

The Golden Rule and empathy are two values that are learned and practiced when students are given opportunities to serve their families, their classmates, their school, and community. Service learning combines both the personal and civic values we talked about earlier in this book. All of the teaching strategies described in this section provide students with opportunities to develop character, to engage in citizenship, to apply their academic skills, and even, in some cases, to find a career.

How Do I Know If the Strategies Are Working?

Evaluation "is the single most powerful way in which teachers communicate their values and beliefs to students, parents, and colleagues."[58]

S. Jeroski, "Finding Out
What We Need to Know," 1992

To help you answer this question, we intend to provide some suggestions that focus on you, your classroom, and your students. (We will leave it to you to use other sources, including what we have written elsewhere on schoolwide character education assessment efforts.[59]) Your efforts to develop the character of your students, to help them learn and practice the core values, is directly related to the environment you create, the relationships you develop, the confidence you inspire, and the expectations you hold for them academically and behaviorally.

Character development of the young is nurtured in the schools and classrooms where students come together to learn, to socialize, to form new relationships, and to practice being caring, cooperative, and compassionate human beings. Evaluation of these and other aspects of classroom life must be seen as snapshots for a child's character development picture book. Part of this book includes pictures about the child's experiences in your classroom with you and his or her classmates. If you were to have a page or two in this picture book, it might include snapshots of your classroom environment, of your teaching abilities, of students' reactions or perceptions about you and the class, about your views, and how others see you as a teacher and character educator.

Asking Questions

Recall the discussion on critical thinking and the value of question asking. Question asking is the camera you will use for evaluating character education efforts as noted in the examples that follow. Remember, though, that the snapshots tell the story. As you analyze them, the story may delight you, concern you, or challenge you. The point is that you are doing an evaluation for two purposes: to find what is working and what is not; to decide what to retain and what to change.

Here are examples of ways to take pictures of yourself, your students, and your classroom. You will have to modify these examples to meet your needs. When assessing students, be sure that the instruments are age-appropriate and at your students' reading levels.

How do your students feel about you and your teaching?

You can use a scale like the one on page 37 with three faces: one smiling, one neutral, and one frowning; or you can use plus and minus signs: ++ really like; + like; – dislike. You should not use all of the items listed at one time. Select those items that meet your initial interests and have the students complete the scale. At some other point you can use the items you didn't use the first time. Don't forget to add items of your own to this list.

Use the results of this scale and the other instruments that follow to get a snapshot of how students perceive you and your effectiveness in teaching the school's core values. What does the picture tell you?

Fill in the following items using these symbols:
++ really like; + like; – dislike
My teacher _____(name):

____Cares about me

____Calls me by my first name

____Helps me do my work

____Listens to me

____Trusts me

____Has confidence in me

____Makes the subject interesting

____Motivates me

____Helps me make good decisions

____Makes me think about my behavior

____Tells when I'm right or wrong and why

____Makes it fun to come to school

____Has interesting things for us to learn

____Has us work in groups

____Holds interesting class meetings

____Helps me and my classmates get along

____Practices what he or she preaches

____Has everyone in this class help one another

____Has us use respectful language

____Grades my work fairly

____Is appreciated by my parents

____Knows a lot about the subjects he or she is teaching

____Expects us to do good work

____Expects us to be respectful and responsible

____Really prepares the lessons he or she teaches

____Makes me think about the choices I make

____Laughs and has fun with us

____Rewards us for doing the right thing

____Wants us to be proud of our class

____Encourages us to ask questions

____Takes many opportunities to teach us values such as courage, honesty, and empathy

____Assigns us interesting projects

____Works with us to do service projects

____Lets us plan some of our own class activities

____Doesn't let us do bad things

____Very seldom scolds us

____Never yells or talks loud

____Makes the classroom neat and cheerful

____Is proud of us and our work

____Rewards us for doing things right

____Add your items_____

Mini-Portfolios

How might you evaluate whether or not your students are learning and practicing one of the core values? If your school has a values-a-month-program, we suggest you try this mini-portfolio idea. On page 40 we have outlined the table of contents and propose that this mini-portfolio be completed by a group of three to four students. We have also included a sample rubric for evaluating it. Courage is the value in this example.

There are many ways to assess portfolio work. Page 41 is an example of a modified rubric from the work of Kay Burke.[60]

Mini-Portfolio: Courage
Table of Contents

1. Definitions

2. Quotations, sayings

3. A book review [fiction]

4. A historical event

5. People in the news

6. Web sites

7. Summary - class discussion

8. Summary - group discussion

9. Interview notes

10. Video or film review

11. Television program review

12. What parents, friends say about courage

13. Our personal experiences

14. Final reflections - what courage means to us

Mini-Portfolio Assessment

To evaluate each team's portfolio, use this rating scale for each of the criteria below:

1 = does not meet expectations

      2 = meets expectations

            3 = exceeds expectations

The comment section is your opportunity to tell the team why they received each rating.

Criteria	Rating	Comments
A. Form (grammar, writing, etc.)	1 2 3	_____
B. Visual appeal	1 2 3	_____
C. Organization	1 2 3	_____
D. Key concepts about the value	1 2 3	_____
E. Understandings of the value	1 2 3	_____
F. Creativity	1 2 3	_____
G. Completeness	1 2 3	_____
H. Depth of reflections	1 2 3	_____
I. Other_____	1 2 3	_____

Teacher Assessment Using Writing

Journals and logs are ways to evaluate the effectiveness of a character education program. Here is an example for using a teacher journal to assess the application of the value, courage, in your classroom. The idea comes from Sagor's booklet on action research. We paraphrase and embellish it here to meet the needs of this example.[61]

Suppose you decided to assess how the value of courage (which is the school value, let us say, for the month of March) is being implemented in your classroom. You decide to spend 10 to 15 minutes after school each day in March recording your responses to the following questions:

- Describe how you tried to teach the value of courage in class today.
- Describe your students' behaviors and interactions regarding this value.
- What worked?
- What did not work?
- What, if anything, surprised you?
- What do you still need to do?
- What do your students need to do?

Save your journal entries. If you had teams of students complete the mini-portfolio, read their work, reflect on your own journal entries, and draw out conclusions about the teaching, learning, and practicing of courage. You may decide to adjust your lesson plans based on what you have learned. These few pages cannot do justice to the time, information, and methods you will need to assess the character education efforts at your school and in your classroom. We offered a few ideas here. We recommend that before engaging in assessment efforts you read the resources in Section IV and visit the Web sites for information.

It is critical to attempt to use the strategies and ideas presented in this section, because students will become more thoughtfully engaged in learning, be more motivated to work hard, and be better able to work together. And, according to the Character Education Partnership, "We know that character education works both from the formal evaluations and assessments that have been made . . . and from the enthusiastic testimony of parents, teachers, principals, and superintendents in districts where character education has been introduced in a serious way."[62]

Curriculum, Activities, and Partnership Questions

How Do I Choose Curriculum and Create Lesson Plans?

> *Where does character education fit into the curriculum? The simple answer is this: everywhere. Since education seeks to help students develop as persons, character development is part and parcel of the whole enterprise.*[63]
>
> K. Ryan and K. Bohlin,
> Building Character in Schools, 1999

Here are a few questions related to curricula that a teacher needs to answer before making decisions.

- How does this curriculum you are considering differ from others?
- Has the curriculum been evaluated?
- What are the findings and the results?
- Will the benefits outweigh the costs? In other words, will the time and money expended on the curriculum yield the results you expect?

- How will you evaluate or assess the curriculum's effectiveness in meeting the expectations (or reaching the outcomes) you have for the program?
- Does the curriculum look like it will engage the students in learning the core values?

Character education is taught through both the content and process of lessons. There are four ways that character education is taught through the curriculum: 1) as a separate subject (e.g., ethics), 2) integrating values thematically through a unit, 3) infusing values into the regular curriculum by focusing on moral issues in the content, and 4) informally, as questions arise.[64]

Separate Lessons on Values

Many schools purchase character education programs that include separate lessons on values. Many of the value lessons are taught when time permits in the classroom. Most publishers recommend daily or weekly lessons specifically devoted to values. We encourage you to try to connect the character education lessons with your regular content lessons, daily classroom activities, and school-wide activities to help students learn the values more holistically. We provide one example.

Literature. One of the most powerful subject areas for teaching values is through literature, both fiction and nonfiction, because "What children read and how they are taught to read can affect the development of good character traits."[65] Discussions and other activities centered around good literature help students develop an appreciation of moral and social issues. And, according to Vincent, stories and literature help students learn, understand, and appreciate the emotions and thoughts of characters from other cultures.[66] Some student outcomes of reading good literature are acquiring a sense of justice and compassion, enhancing their moral imagination and moral sensibility as they vicariously experience the lives of characters, and having a storehouse of moral models to guide their actions.[67]

Here is an example of how literature is used in one school. Let's call it Lincoln School. The Character Education Committee (CEC) decided to teach the school's nine core values by implementing a

"Value-a-Month-Literacy-Program" (VAMLP).[68] Values were taught through "reading" during Lincoln's three-hour literacy block. Grade-appropriate literature illustrating the core values was made available to all teachers in the school library. Lincoln's principal purchased multiple copies of the books chosen by the staff for the VAMLP to be used in each classroom.

The VAMLP contained a number of procedures. First, a book was assigned on a schoolwide level each month. Second, each class read and discussed each story and responded to the literature in their own way. Third, each class displayed responses to the assigned literature throughout the school. Fourth, at the end of each month, an assembly dedicated to the monthly value was held. Assemblies highlighted examples of real-life situations that related to the value of the month. In addition, monthly family literacy nights encouraged parent involvement.

Other Programs. In addition to literature, here is just a sampling of prepared programs that contain separate value lessons: "Lessons in Character" by Young Peoples' Press, Character Education Institute Curriculum, Elkind & Sweet Communications/Livewire Video Programs, The Institute for Global Ethics' "Ethical Fitness Program," and Quest International Programs. Do some exploring on your own (see Section IV). One of the best Web sites for information about prepared programs and ratings on character education programs is www.character.org.

We close this topic by sharing some of our teaching tips for using separate lessons on character education:

- Try to match your lessons with the expectations and outcomes of the school's character education program.
- Incorporate, adapt, or connect the character lessons with your existing content lessons, when possible.
- Make adaptations to the lessons to ensure they are developmentally appropriate and intrinsically motivating for diverse groups of students.
- Use the teacher guide and any supplementary materials/resources to select questions, classroom activities, strategies for parents, and assessment criteria.

- Go beyond the individual lesson and provide a context for students to apply the core values. Try having your students put the values into practice (e.g., hands-on activities, cooperative group processing with peers, and community service learning).

Integrate Values Thematically into a Unit

Thematic units provide connections for students across content areas that are very supportive of a deeper understanding of values, because students see how the values are integrated into the different subjects. Thematic units foster connections between students and content, students and teachers, and students and students. We highly recommend a thematic approach.

Here is one example, provided by one of our master's program students, who is a parent volunteer and a teacher at the Pearson School in Modesto, California.[69] She is one of the two kindergarten teachers that are implementing the BEST program in their diverse classrooms. Building Esteem in Students Today (BEST) is a school-wide character education program comprising nine values for each grade level. BEST claims to:

- Teach tolerance, courtesy, and respect for others
- Increase teaching time
- Include parent involvement
- Reduce disruptive behavior
- Maintain the existing curriculum
- Save money (e.g., student worksheets are included and no training is required)
- Improve peer relationships through interactive activities
- Combine character development efforts of home, school, and community
- Promote care of community/school property and improve school climate [70]

A different theme is introduced for each monthly value. The BEST value themes and unit objectives are:

- Conflict and Feelings: Conflict Resolution, Communication Skills. The objective is to focus on conflict resolution and decision making.

47

- Responsibility: Citizenship, Decision-making Skills, Reliability/Accountability. The objective is to give students the opportunity to practice skills in decision making and consequences of actions.
- Courtesy: Respect for Others/Self, Fairness/Kindness. The objective is to reinforce the importance of being considerate and respectful and to set the tone for manners.
- Goal Setting: Initiative/Self-discipline, Career Development. The objective is for students to set personal goals, create situations for success, and create a classroom climate in which children are free to overcome the fear of failure.
- Honesty: Integrity, Truthfulness, Trust. The objective is to promote fairness, truthfulness, and honest behavior.
- Caring and Sharing: Regarding Others, Serving Others/Community. The objective is to develop healthy self-esteem by caring for others.
- Positive Classroom: Setting Expectations, Attentiveness/Listening Skills, Positive Climate. The objective is to promote a positive, affirming school atmosphere from the first day of school.
- Esteem: Acceptance of Differences, Recognizing Strengths/Talents. The objective is for students to recognize their strengths and praise them for exhibiting positive values (emphasis on belonging, competence, and worth).
- Health and Prevention: Drug and Alcohol Abuse, Dealing with Stress. The objective is to discuss the importance of having a healthy attitude, and discuss healthy and safe living.[71]

Each unit in the BEST program includes a wide variety of messages, activities, and a bibliography. In addition to schoolwide activities, each unit directly involves each classroom by suggesting value activities for teachers. Individual teachers and students work on learning the values simultaneously. Posters about the value are displayed at the beginning of each unit. Each day, students recite positive messages about the value and adults promote the value through modeling and praise. Each week there is a 10- to 30-minute classroom activity selected to promote the value. Each unit has a teacher guide and suggestions for parents and community activities and projects. Teachers send home a parent newsletter at the start of each unit to get the family involved in promoting the value. Finally, all staff members receive a newsletter that encourages them to model value-related behavior.

The BEST Program was developed by educators to build student character, values, and citizenship without curriculum changes. Next, we describe how to infuse values into the regular curriculum by making adjustments to your existing lessons.

Infuse Values into the Regular Curriculum

Infusing values into the regular curriculum is the preferred method for educating for character. Integrating values makes character education more than an add-on, it teaches values more holistically and helps students apply the core values to everything they study and do. The content of the curriculum naturally has rich ethical and value issues and concepts for students to study. You can mine the values in any subject area by having students use higher-order thinking to analyze the content. Lickona recommends that we "analyze each subject (e.g., social studies, science, English) asking the question, What are the values and ethical issues in the material I teach?"[72]

A teacher in the Ramona Unified School District (RUSD) in California would find that her district's content standards for history-social science K–12 identify a character education standard. The standard reads: "These [eight] traits and their related qualities are to be taught within the context of the existing academic curriculum rather than as an additional and isolated subject."[73] One of the eight specific values chosen by the district is responsibility. Responsibility is defined as being accountable for one's decisions and actions and the consequences of those actions. The RUSD has a resources guide for teachers, "Resources for Teaching Civic Values," that includes ideas, activities, and literature titles to use with lessons. The resource guide gives these recommendations for integrating the value of responsibility into lessons (this is a modified list for elementary teachers):

- Discuss the difference between being responsible and irresponsible related to your math homework. Brainstorm several ideas. Select groups of students to create skits demonstrating the different behaviors. Then, debrief the skits.
- Establish behavioral norms with your class.
- Establish classroom responsibilities so students have opportunities to put this value into practice.
- Make a booklet for science entitled, "My responsibilities with the classroom pets." Students can feature a picture or drawing with a short description of a responsibility on each page.[74]

Informally Teach Values as Situations Arise

You may prefer not to teach formal lessons on values but instead wait for situations to arise, or questions to be posed, and then pause and take time to discuss the value, or priorities, or ethical aspects of an event/issue at hand. As the classroom teacher, you can take advantage of "teachable moments," when you can discuss issues and events with students as they arise in your classroom. Ideally, you want to become the type of teacher that students say "live and breathe" the values you are asking students to follow. In this way, you will be a model of character education and, because of this, the students will want to emulate you (see Section II).

If you are informally teaching values, you do so while going about the daily routine of teaching. Informal teaching of values occurs in many classrooms. Some teachers are not even aware that they are using a powerful method to teach children positive personal and prosocial character traits. A lot of these informal strategies are those that any effective teacher would use, such as allowing students to make choices, facilitating students working together, discussing issues related to an event that occurred on the playground, and asking questions to help students feel empathy for others and understand the reasons for their actions. Character education objectives can be met by engaging students in these methods.

Use Informal and Formal Methods

We believe that there is both a need for being explicit about teaching values and a need for using informal approaches to teach values. For a long time, individual classroom teachers worked in individual classrooms, teaching students positive personal and prosocial values through the classroom activities and climate. Teachers can no longer afford to be so casual about character education. Section I of this book established the need for more direct, formal, imbedded, and contextual lessons that connect directly to character education goals and objectives. A teacher can no longer be satisfied to use only an informal approach. The strongest exemplars of character education are teachers who blend both the informal teaching and formal teaching strategies into their content lessons. Following are teaching tips for integrating character informally and formally into lessons:

- Seize the teachable moments.
- Go deep into the content by using higher-order thinking strategies.
- Apply the 8 Cs (see Section II).
- Extend learning to involve activities at home and in the community.
- Include a character building objective in each lesson plan.

The basic premise for your selection of a character education curriculum is captured in the words "infusion" and "integration." Character education should not be considered an add-on. It needs to be a critical part of the existing school curricular and co-curricular programs. It needs to be integrated into the daily life of the classroom and school. It needs to be part of the school's partnership efforts with parents and community members. To date the most popular character education programs are literature-based programs and Value-a-Month-Programs. Whichever your school decides to use, we urge you to use the questions we posed at the beginning of this section (pages 44-45).

What About Schoolwide and Co-Curricular Activities?

Activity programs are the perfect complement to the class-room—not because students learn how to become more proficient in sports or debate or music, but because they learn how to become productive citizens in these hands-on laboratories.[75]

R. Kanaby, "Willing Learners Remove
Apathy from the Equation," 1996

As a teacher concerned about the character development of students, there are some things you should know about the benefits of co-curricular and schoolwide activities that support the core values fostered by the school and nurtured in your classroom.

Several components in a school's comprehensive character education initiatives, such as schoolwide and community-based activities, curriculum and classroom activities, and co-curricular and service activities need the attention of you, the CEC, and other stakeholders. For example, research shows that students who participate in co-curricular activities (from clubs to sports) are less likely to drop out of school, have higher aspirations, and have a sense of belonging to the school.

Participation in the school's activities program contributes to citizenship and social skill development, and in many cases, to academic achievement.[76] But students have to be introduced to and encouraged to participate in these activities. Your role, then, is to encourage students to get involved in schoolwide activities and in co-curricular programs (many may already be involved in community activities—particularly sports programs—so use these to get the students to reflect on their experiences). Encouragement is one thing, but you should also provide students with in-class experiences to help them take leadership roles, learn to speak before groups, learn listening skills, learn the value of teamwork, and learn how to apply the school's core values to their activities. This invitation and the introductory experiences begin in your classroom under your tutelage and guidance.

Schoolwide Activities and Testimonials

It is not our intent to provide a list of all possible schoolwide activities that support character development efforts. We intend to list a few, with quotes from principals of award-winning character education schools, and assume that you will visit Section IV of this book for additional information and ideas. A few suggestions will give you a "picture" of what other schools are doing.

- Citizen-of-the-week programs, certificates of behavior, good character awards
- Daily school television programs that have a segment on the value of the month
- Monthly school assemblies produced by students
- Fund-raising and donation programs
- School motto, rules, core values posters, banners, displays
- Parent and community support—money, talent, time—for schoolwide activities
- After-school PTA-run programs and activities for students that support the values
- Visits by business and community members talking about their work, skills needed, expectations, what it takes to be a good employee, and professional ethics
- Family service programs offered by individuals and agencies in the community
- Adopt-a-family program
- Life skills program for all students focusing on manners and social skills
- Multicultural thematic units connecting history, literature, health, culture, customs, traditions, and foods
- Weekly and daily "character conversations" emanating from "teachable moments" related to school and community problems, issues, and concerns
- Monthly calendar featuring each of the values of the month and daily activities on things to do to practice each value
- Field trips to senior service centers, homeless shelters, hospitals, and nursing homes
- Teamwork and leadership training for students

- Community service projects
- Character clubs, councils, publications, and events
- Monthly student publication about character and the value of the month
- Behavior code contract

We leave you with these quotes from principals of award-winning schools as exemplars of their reflection on the power and impact of character education on the teachers and their diverse students.

> *We got caught up in recognition initially. We soon realized it was taking away from internal motivation. We do not do awards and rewards anymore. We help students to be reflective. We encourage teachers to respond to what students write about and do; the reinforcement is personal.*[77]

> *When you deal with this much diversity, you need a common language, and the language of universal values cuts across all cultures.*[78]

> *We have the power to build or preserve ideals among young children and sustain their sense of wonder about the world. Whether it is the beauty of language, the fascination with nature, or the heroism of man, it is for us to sustain a child's belief in the ultimate goodness of the world. If we let that belief slip away from children, what have we left them?*[79]

Classroom Projects

For the young, developing the skills and talents to participate in schoolwide character education efforts begins in the classroom. It starts with classroom projects that you and your students create. To this end, we offer you a "project checklist" on page 56. The purpose of the checklist is to have you reflect on what a particular project contributes to student character development. We suggest you modify this checklist to meet your needs. While the checklist is for your reflection, it may be modified so students can use it to assess the extent to which a project contributed to their development.

To gather more information about the importance of a project to you, or the students, or both, in a class discussion, you could ask the "how" question after each item. A similar checklist can also be used to assess schoolwide activities. For example, the "stem" (incomplete sentence) at the top of the checklist on page 56 might read: "This community service project contributed to the students using some or all of the items listed." (How?) Or, the "stem" might read: "This schoolwide activity provided the students with a sense of caring for other students." (How?) The idea, which you know very well by now, is to create projects, tasks, and assignments that foster the school's core values, underscoring each project or activity with reflective thinking about the contribution the project makes to the students' knowledge, skills, and development of values.

Project Checklist

This project _____ contributed to some
name of project
extent [greatly or moderately] to my students':

_____ Knowledge of the subject, topic, or issue

_____ Leadership skills

_____ Citizenship skills

_____ Understanding of the values (name them)

_____ Application of the values (name them)

_____ Creativity

_____ Critical thinking skills (which one in particular)

_____ Teamwork skills

_____ Social skills (which ones)

_____ Relationships with adults

_____ Relationships with peers

_____ Problem-solving skills

_____ Decision-making skills

_____ Time management skills

How Can I Involve Parents and the Community?

> *The long-term success of (character) education depends on forces outside the school—on the extent to which families and communities join schools in a common effort to meet the needs of children and foster their healthy development.*[80]

T. Lickona,
Educating for Character, 1991

No school and no teacher can develop the character of children alone. It does take a "village." That village is a community that includes families, neighborhoods, adult relationships, and peer groups; the media and marketplace; as well as the Internet, television, movies, and video games. For most children, character education is a continuum of time, relationships, and experiences that occur in the home, school, and community. It is the tasks of educators, in schools, to bring these institutions together to help each other teach children and youth to know and do good things, to practice the core values in the community, and to learn to be active and contributing citizens in a democracy.

Much has been written on the importance of parent and community involvement in the education of the young. No doubt you are well aware that the research indicates that parent involvement in the education of a child has a positive influence on that child's academic achievement and attitudes.[81] You and your colleagues probably employ an array of activities for involving parents and the community in the daily life of the school and in the education of each child.

Our intent in answering the question of parent and community involvement is to provide you with ideas for inviting and involving families and community members in the character education of the children at your school. So, over the next few pages, we offer you some tried-and-true ideas, suggestions, and recommendations.

Community Group Partnership Ideas

> *Schools must recognize and acknowledge the unique char-*
> *acteristics of the community; design programs to build*
> *strengths and needs of the community; seek opportunities*
> *to engage and invite the community to participate in*
> *school activities; and use a variety of strategies to com-*
> *municate directly with the community.*[82]
>
> B. Rutherford and S. Billig,
> "Eight Lessons of Parent, Family,
> and Community Involvement," 1995

When we say community, we refer to the numerous businesses, civic organizations, youth agencies, service clubs, not-for-profit groups, and community leaders who can and should get involved in supporting home and school character education efforts. Here are a dozen home and school partnership ideas for community involvement:

1. Provide service opportunities for students.
2. Support a speakers' bureau.
3. Promote the core values within your organization.
4. Highlight the importance of character on community bulletin boards, in malls, in business ads, and in commercials.
5. Display student work on character.
6. Adopt a school, and provide models, mentors, and tutors.
7. Support and contribute to publications on character and character education.
8. Establish community character award programs recognizing citizens (adults and youth) for service, leadership, and exemplary character.
9. Offer training about character and ethics within the organization.
10. Provide employees a half-day per month to go to schools and work with students or perform other tasks at school.
11. Support library efforts to purchase literature that offers students both fiction and nonfiction stories about character.
12. Form a single leadership committee whose task is to

promote character and ethics throughout the community.

School Partnership Activities

> *A starting point for any effort to improve the character of our youth is the realization that good character is not inherited; it must be taught. In the home, in the classroom, in religious institutions, and in the community, adults must deliberately and diligently teach what it means to a be a person of good character.*[83]
>
> H. R. LeGette,
> Parents, Kids, and Character, 1999

There are many useful schoolwide partnership suggestions in publications and in practice that are designed to engage parents and community members in the school's character education initiatives. Following are ten suggestions gleaned from what your colleagues are doing in schools across the United States (see Section IV). Consider this list an idea generator to be used by you and your school colleagues.

1. Remind all adults who come into contact with children in and out of the school that the best way to foster the core values is to model them.
2. Encourage parents and community members to work with the school in helping children make "connections" between character and their future success in the workplace.
3. Promote a "culture of character and core values" in the home, school, and community.
4. Provide service opportunities in the school, classroom, home, and community.
5. Offer school personnel, parents, and community members training opportunities about character education.
6. Encourage adults and organizations in the community to work with the school in strengthening positive peer group relationships, including training in peer mediation and conflict resolution.
7. Plaster the school with pictures of heroes and heroines, with character sayings and quotations, and with definitions of

core values, and provide some of these for parents to post on their refrigerators.

8. Invite parents, grandparents, and other adults to the school to talk with students at assemblies and in classrooms about their personal, heroic, and courageous experiences.

9. Invite parents and the community to the school to celebrate, recognize, and reward students for their talents, achievements, and good character.

10. Ask parents and others to help the school reinforce the use of proper, respectful language and manners.

Classroom Partnership Activities

> *To maintain ongoing applications of the traits/values learned, it is important to create and maintain a school and classroom environment where positive behavior and attitudes are continuously discussed and promoted. Charts, logs, and journals are examples of ways to keep track of student progress on applying the lessons learned. This program is not a stand-alone program predicated on isolated lessons. The lessons learned are to be considered a life skill to be practiced and applied each day in all areas of school: recess, lunch, assemblies, and the classroom.*[84]
>
> Lowell Joint School District (California),
> Character Education Program Manual

You know well the tried-and-true Open House Night. Parents and guardians come to your classroom, sit in the children's seats, and listen to your presentation about the curriculum and content standards for your grade level and/or subject. Then they listen to your commentary about children's responsibilities and your recital about classroom rules and procedures. They hear your list of expectations for their children and how they can help. The session ends with questions and answers and then off everyone goes to the cafeteria for snacks.

How about having "Character Night" or, at the very least, include character education information in your "Open House Night" talk. With character education added, "Open House Night" becomes more than telling parents what children will learn. It engages the parents in understanding how children will apply the school's core values, how they will be expected to behave, how behavior and achievement are related, and how and why support from the home is essential. It educates them about how the school's core values are translated into the curriculum and the daily activities in your classroom.

The first step is to prepare your classroom character education plan. We have observed unanimous support by parents to a character education program when each teacher provides a clear, well-developed rationale for how they are going to teach the school's core values in his or her classroom. We recommend that you prepare this in writing to distribute during "Character Night" or "Open House Night" and be ready to provide updates and highlights about character education lessons and activities to parents throughout the year in a section of your class newspaper or class Web site. Here are some ideas for a classroom character education plan:

- In our classroom this year, our classroom rules and procedures support the school's core values of responsibility, respect, fairness, and so on. Everyone is expected to follow the class rules and procedures we established during the first week of school.
- Our class rewards, as well as consequences, are based on the school's core values.
- Our lessons will highlight the values and ethics related to all the subject areas we study this year: in history, in literature, in science lab activities, and in math applications (give some examples here).
- Our whole-class and group activities will focus on prosocial values (positive behaviors), so we all learn how to work together to complete tasks.

The second step is to present your plan to parents during "Character Night" or "Open House Night." Ribas, an assistant superintendent, has collected strategies to help teachers make successful parent presentations.[85] We include a modification of his ideas here because we think that they will help you make a better presentation of your classroom character education plan to parents.

- Practice making your presentation and discuss it with your colleagues.
- Provide an outline of your character education plan for each parent so he or she can follow along.
- Be organized, clear, concise, and cordial, and use a conversational tone.
- Be a "techie"—use Powerpoint, a slide show, or videos, or simply rely on the overhead projector with colorful, informative transparencies.
- If the district has a parent handbook, know its contents, particularly that which refers to the values being promoted by the district or school.
- Anticipate difficult questions in advance, particularly those relating to behavior and character and the core values.
- Try to answer negative questions with positive answers. Don't be intimidated; be professional.
- If you don't know the answer to a question, admit it, tell parents you'll find the answer, and move on.
- Leave time at the end of your presentation for questions and comments from the parents.
- Arrange for ways your parents can be contacted, discussing what time and methods are best for them (written notes, e-mail, phone calls).
- Have a sign-up sheet ready for parents who want to meet with you privately.
- Provide handouts about character and character education that parents can take with them when they leave.

Parents will need reassurance that their efforts to raise their children to become responsible adults are being supported in your classroom. Baker's research on teacher perceptions of parent involvement contains useful suggestions for involving parents in your classroom and in children's academic and character education.[86] With some modifications, we summarize her findings for you to help improve your efforts to involve parents in your classroom. In your interactions with the parents, work to:

- Create a relationship that promotes both you and parents working toward the same objectives. In character education, those objectives are the ones that specify the school's core values and the goals of the program.
- Find ways to encourage parents to come to your classroom as often as possible to observe their children, and to work with students under your direction.
- Convince parents to get involved in children's homework but not do it for them. Parents must create the time and atmosphere so that a child can get homework done (responsibility modeled, responsibility learned).
- Encourage parents to read to their children the rich multicultural literature about people that do and do not foster the core values of the school and then engage in conversations about these characters.
- Remind parents to supervise what their children watch on television, their use of the Internet, and the content of movies and video games.
- Encourage parents to teach their child the core values and social skills so that it reinforces what is being done in your classroom and around the school.
- Encourage parents to come to your classroom to discuss their work and work habits and to be models for your students.
- Create class projects that require parent/guardian participation to help children see that what happens at school and at home are connected.
- Work with parents to help them overcome barriers that prevent them from coming to your classroom (language, transportation, child care, schedules, etc.).

You, the teacher, need to work with parents on the character development of their children. We cannot emphasize enough, how important it is that parents know you are their partner and that you share similar goals. As LeGette tells us, "Parents are the primary transmitters of values to children, and it is they who bear the major responsibility for teaching what it means to be a moral person."[87]

Parents, along with community members, need to be invited, welcomed, and engaged in classroom activities and projects, because it is the entire community that has the largest stake in the outcome—children becoming good citizens.

Resources

Published Books

Boyer, E. L. *The Basic School: A Community of Learners.* Princeton, NJ: The Carnegie Foundation for the Advancement of Teaching, 1995.

> This book describes the "basic school" as it takes the push for school renewal back to the first years of formal learning and back to each local school where all teaching and learning occurs. It is basic because it gives priority to language and proposes a coherent curriculum. It is basic because it identifies the proven components of an effective education and brings them all together. The book presents a comprehensive, practical plan of action based on best practices for elementary and middle schools.

Broome, S. A., and Henley, N. W. *Teaching Character. . . It's Elementary: 36 Weeks of Daily Lessons for Grades K–5.* Chapel Hill, NC: Character Development Publishing, 2000.

> Read about and use the character lessons of two elementary teachers with more than 45 years of experience. Daily lessons described in an easy-to-use lesson format focus on such values as honesty, fairness, kindness, and responsibility. The lessons can be easily

incorporated into daily classroom lessons and the curriculum. The format includes a goal, an array of activities, materials needed, and evaluation ideas.

Dalton, J., and Watson, M. *Among Friends: Classrooms Where Caring and Learning Prevail.* Oakland, CA: Developmental Studies Center, 1997.

This is an excellent resource for ideas on how to put guiding principles for character education to work in classrooms. Explicit and concrete methods are described and models are shared. The teachers described in the book all integrate their own version of the "four keys to classroom community": 1) building kind and respectful relationships with and among students, 2) being explicit about teaching humane values, 3) drawing upon students' internal motivation to learn and to contribute, and 4) teaching in ways that support students' active construction of knowledge. This book is foundational for all elementary and middle level teachers.

DeRoche, E., and Williams, M. *Educating Hearts and Minds: A Comprehensive Character Education Framework,* 2nd ed. Thousand Oaks, CA: Corwin Press, 2001.

This second edition merges new ideas in character education research with best practices in schools and districts. The authors provide the most up-to-date and comprehensive framework for K–12 administrators, educators, and concerned citizens. It offers easy access to practical and proven methods supported by an in-depth rationale. The authors propose standards, promising practices, and assessment instruments that can be personalized to fit the needs and interests of any school, district, or community. For more information, go to http://teachvalues.org.

Devine, T., HoSeuk, J., and Wilson, A. *Cultivating Heart and Character: Educating for Life's Most Essential Goals.* New York: International Educational Foundation, 2000.

This book reflects the experience and assistance of educators and experts from a variety of backgrounds from all around the world. It provides a cross-cultural perspective. Incorporating both meaning and method, this book will interest anyone who cares about a better future and the people who will help create it. Some of the questions addressed include: Why does character education need to be a priority in schools and families? What universal principles inform moral growth and healthy relationships? How can schools and parents forge viable partnerships with communities to provide children with the assets they need to live fulfilled and useful lives? For more information, go to http://www.cultivatingheartandcharacter.com.

Jacobs, D., and Jacobs-Spencer, J. *Teaching Virtues: Building Character Across the Curriculum.* Lanham, MD: Scarecrow Press, 2001.

The authors present an approach that does not separate character education from effective teaching but instead makes it foundational. Classroom teachers will find the teaching strategies and ideas for integrating character content in each subject matter area to be useful and practical. The authors' checklist for integrating character into every lesson is a valuable resource. After reading this book, you will be convinced that effective character education should not be a supplemental activity.

Kirschenbaum, H. *100 Ways to Enhance Values and Morality in School and Youth Settings.* Boston: Allyn and Bacon, 1995.

This book presents a comprehensive approach to values and moral education. It draws on the best of the approaches and the methods that have worked for centuries and those that have been developed in recent decades to help young people grow up with clear values, good character, moral integrity, and the knowledge and skills to be good citizens. The combination of traditional and new approaches makes this book unique. The practical approaches are described with clear guidelines, examples, and suggestions for implementation.

LeGette, H. *Parents, Kids and Character: 21 Strategies to Help Your Children Develop Good Character.* Chapel Hill, NC: Character Development Publishing, 1999.

The strategies offered in this book grew out of Dr. LeGette's work as an associate school superintendent in North Carolina, where she worked with parents, educators, board members, and representatives of community agencies in planning and implementing a character education project. A group of parents asked for some recommendations. The 21 strategies were a part of the resource material she compiled for the parents. This book is a practical resource guide for parents.

Lickona, T. *Educating for Character: Teaching Respect and Responsibility.* New York: Bantam Books, 1991.

In this seminal text, the author discusses the need for and ways to develop schools and classrooms that are civil, respectful, caring, and responsible. Dr. Lickona offers a character education model that provides school and classroom examples, useful suggestions, and practical strategies. It is a "must read" for all who care about developing the character of children and youth by being role models, mentors, and caregivers. He writes about teaching values in a democratic classroom environment, the importance of class meetings and cooperative learning, moral conversations and reflections, caring classrooms, and the need for a moral school culture.

Ryan, K., and Bohlin, K. *Building Character in Schools.* San Francisco, CA: Jossey-Bass, 1999.

The authors capitalized on their experiences as character educators to write this comprehensive book on character education in schools and communities. The initial chapters make the case for character education; then the authors describe ways to build a school as a community of virtues. Chapters are devoted to infusing character content in the curriculum and the life of the school, engaging and involving parents, finding ways to solicit student participation, and giving special attention to teachers and their role for nurturing character in their classrooms. The appendices provide valuable ideas, strategies, and resources.

Urban, H. *Life's Greatest Lessons or 20 Things I Want My Kids to Know.* Redwood City, CA: Great Lessons Press, 1997.

Motivational speaker Hal Urban's book reflects his personal and professional experiences raising three boys as a single father and more than 30 years teaching high school students. In *Life's Greatest Lessons*, he describes 20 things young people should know about life and living, successes and failures, and character and virtues. But this is not just a book for teenagers. Its popularity among adults is testimony that the ideas and suggestions transcend age and experience. This small book is filled with "big" ideas—lessons for being good and doing good.

Vincent, P. *Promising Practices in Character Education.* Chapel Hill, NC: Character Development Group, 1998.

Dr. Vincent is a storyteller who describes what is happening in

nine schools with character education programs that hope to pro-
duce caring, responsible, and respectful citizens. In this volume,
he reports on real-life stories that demonstrate how effective character education programs are thriving in schools of all sizes and
varying demographics. The stories provide important clues, practical strategies, and useful ideas for careful planning, proper
implementation, and evaluation. (Note: Volume 2 offers 12 new
school success stories.)

Wiley, L. *Comprehensive Character-Building Classroom: A Handbook for
Teachers*. DeBary, FL: Longwood Communications, 1998.

Dr. Wiley's book began as part of her doctoral dissertation. She
provides a theoretical orientation to character education from the
research, presenting both psychological and philosophical points
of view. She defines character, describes how children learn character, and provides a rationale for why it is important. The body
of the book centers around six categories, which, the author maintains, encompass all aspects of a comprehensive character-building classroom (leadership, climate, community, correction, curriculum, and common projects). The book concludes with methods of assessing the character of students.

School and Classroom Programs

Basic School Network, University of Missouri-Columbia, 202 Hill Hall,
Columbia, MO 65211; Tel: (816) 235-2454, Fax: (816) 235-6511,
http://basicschool.coe.missouri.edu/

The Basic School Network represents the original school-based
practitioners trained and commissioned by Ernest L. Boyer.
Network practice is based on Boyer's 1995 report, *The Basic School:
A Community for Learning*. The report focuses on four priorities for
school renewal: The School as Community, A Curriculum with
Coherence, A Climate for Learning, and A Commitment to
Character. The Network was identified by the U.S.D.E. as 1 of 17
programs recommended for Title 1/Porter-Obey funding initiatives. Regional Centers offer a consistent array of services and training institutes to schools and districts across the nation and abroad.

Character Counts! Program, Josephson Institute of Ethics, 4640
Admiralty Way, Suite 1001, Marina del Ray, CA 90292-6610; Tel:
(310) 306-1868, Fax: (310) 827-1864, http://www.character-
counts.org

The six pillars of character upon which this school-community character education program is based include trustworthiness, respect, responsibility, fairness, caring, and citizenship. Operated by the Josephson Institute of Ethics and endorsed by a large coalition of educational, civic, and youth-serving agencies, program offerings include character development seminars, community awareness workshops, educator in-service programs, and training for teachers working with high-risk youth.

CHARACTERplus, 8225 Florissant Road, St. Louis, MO 63121; Tel: (314) 692-9728 or (800) 478-5684, Fax: (314) 516-4599, http://info.csd.org/staffdev/chared/characterplus.html

The mission of CHARACTERplus is based on the tenet that within the cultural diversity of schools there is a core set of values that all share. CHARACTERplus models, teaches, and communicates these shared beliefs and values, which are responsibility, respect, humanity, honesty, self-esteem and cooperation. As a result, students will adopt these beliefs and values as a part of their personal ethics and become positive contributors to society. The program deals with civic education, school-based programs, service learning, and staff development. They also focus on conflict resolution, life/social skills, and moral reasoning. CHARACTERplus hosts a national character education conference annually in St. Louis, Missouri.

Child Development Project, Developmental Studies Center, 2000 Embarcadero, Suite 305, Oakland, CA 94606-5300; Tel: (510) 533-0213, Fax: (510) 464-3670, http://www.devstu.org

The Child Development Project (CDP) is endorsed by the National Association of Elementary School Principals. The intent of the program is to create a "caring community of learners" in classrooms and in schools. The classroom component of the program includes a literature-based approach to reading and language arts, coupled with a cooperative learning emphasis, and classroom management and discipline practices that develop the class as a caring community of learners. The second component of the program includes an array of schoolwide activities and events. The third component is a family involvement program that is closely coordinated with the school curriculum and schoolwide events.

Community of Caring, 1325 G Street, NW, Washington, DC 20005; Tel: (202) 393-1251, Fax: (202) 824-0351, www.communityofcaring.org

The Community of Caring program is a project of the Joseph F. Kennedy, Jr., Foundation and is endorsed by the National Association of Secondary School Principals. The project works to promote and encourage five values in schools using a total community approach: caring, respect, responsibility, trust, and family. Program offerings include teacher training, student value discussions and forums, family involvement, and community service opportunities for students.

Elkind & Sweet Communications/Livewire Video, 3450 Sacramento Street, San Francisco, CA 94118; Tel: (415) 759-3904, Fax: (415) 665-8006, www.goodcharacter.com or www.livewiremedia.com

Elkind & Sweet produces such video-based programs as *The Power of Choice* (Grades 6–12), *Big Changes, Big Choices* (Grades 5–9), and *You Can Choose!* (Grades 1–4) to help young people discover that they have the power of choice, are responsible for the choices they make, and owe it to themselves to make the best choices.

The Giraffe Project, P.O. Box 759, 197 Second Street, Langley, WA 98260; Tel: (360) 221-7989, Fax: (360) 221-7817, http://www.giraffe.org

The Giraffe Project is designed to seek out people with vision and courage who have made a change in some way and to tell their stories to the public and in schools so that it will encourage others to stick their necks out. Through its heroes program, the GP offers educators a story-based curriculum that teaches the values of courage, compassion, and citizenship. Included in the GP are teacher guides for grades K–2, 3–5, and 6–9. The guides and newsletters feature stories on real-life heroes and ways students can be involved in service projects.

The Heartwood Ethics Institute, 425 North Craig Street, Suite 302, Pittsburgh, PA 15213; Tel: (800) HEART 10, Fax: (412) 688-8570, www.heartwoodethics.org

The Heartwood Ethics Institute's curriculum for elementary school children is a literature-based character education program. Teachers receive a multicultural reading kit filled with beautifully written and illustrated books that include folk and hero stories, legends, and contemporary tales. The content of each grade-level kit contains seven universal concepts: courage, loyalty, justice, respect, hope, honesty, and love. The kit also includes lesson cards for each book, a resource manual, flags, and a world map addressing the location of each of the stories.

The Institute for Global Ethics, 11/13 Main Street, P.O. Box 563, Camden, ME 04843; Tel: (207) 236-6658, Fax: (207) 236-4014, http://www.globalethics.org

IGE's vision is for "a world where shared moral values shape relationships, determine decisions, and guide the actions for every individual, institution, and nation." The IGE mission is to promote public discourse and practical action around significant ethical issues by 1) discovering and defining the global common ground of shared values; 2) establishing clear structures for moral reasoning and ethical decision making; 3) promoting the teaching of *ethical fitness* in the practices of private, institutional, and civic virtue; 4) analyzing trends, gathering and disseminating information, and developing new knowledge about global ethics; and 5) being a model organization in effectiveness, outreach, efficiency, and ethical action.

Quest International, 1984 Coffman Road, P.O. Box 4850, Newark, OH 43058-4850; Tel: (614) 522-9165, http://www.quest.edu

Supported by Lions Clubs throughout the world, endorsed by several educational organizations, and with some research support, Quest International (QI) offers a variety of curriculum and instructional materials for teachers and students at all grade levels. The K—5 program is called *Skills for Growing,* 6–8 is *Skills for Adolescence,* and 9–12 is *Skills for Action.* Life skills, character education, drug prevention, violence prevention, and service learning are its major emphases. QI offers education professional development workshops, evaluation assistance, and youth advocacy presentations.

School Development Program, Yale Child Study Center, 55 College Street, New Haven, CT 06510; Tel: (203) 737-1020, Fax: (203) 737-1023, http://pandora.med.yale.edu/comer/welcome.html

Led by James Comer from the Yale University Child Study Center, the School Development Program is a systemic school reform strategy based on child, adolescent, and adult development principles with a focus on strengthening students' holistic development and academic success. The program is designed to help educators and community members create management teams that use three guiding principles (no-fault, consensus, collaboration) and three school operation methods (planning, staff development, and assessment).

Southern Poverty Law Center, 400 Washington Ave., Montgomery, AL 36104; Tel: (334) 264-0286, Fax: (334) 264-3121, http://www.splcenter.org/teachingtolerance/tt-index.html

Teaching Tolerance, the education project of the Southern Poverty Law Center, provides teachers at all levels with the resources and ideas for promoting interracial and intercultural understanding in the classroom. The program stresses the importance of teaching children respect and appreciation for each other. To help achieve this goal, it distributes curriculum tools and a semi-annual magazine, at low or no cost, that offer teachers ready-to-use ideas and strategies based on the premises that tolerance is at the core of good citizenship, can be taught, and belongs everywhere in the curriculum.

WiseSkills, P.O. Box 491, Santa Cruz, CA 95061; Tel: (888)-WISESKILLS (1-888-947-3754), Fax: (831) 426-8930, http://www.wiseskills.com

WiseSkills is a comprehensive, interdisciplinary character education program that highlights the words and lives of great world figures. WiseSkills focuses on three critical areas: character education, career awareness, and community service. The program includes a teacher-friendly K–8 classroom curriculum along with optional parent/community involvement activities. The program strengthens students' character through a variety of interconnected activities and experiences.

Organizations

We understand that Web site links, along with phone numbers and addresses, change over time. To ensure that the links are current, we direct you to the ICCE Web site at the University of San Diego for frequent updates: http://teachvalues.org. You can bookmark the ICCE Web site to use it to click through to the character education organizations listed here.

Argus Communications
P.O. Box 9550
400 West Bethany Drive, Suite 110
Allen, TX 75013-9550
Tel: (800) 860-6762
Fax: (800) 243-5299
http://www.argus.com/index.htm

Argus is dedicated to being the leader in providing quality, relevant, message-based products that help people express themselves and touch the lives of others. Argus creates products that add to the quality of life by uplifting, encouraging, and inspiring people. Argus is best known for its motivational, inspirational, and educational products, including posters, banners, Pass It On Message Cards, greeting cards, T-shirts, and gift items. Argus maintains its historical commitment to education, particularly to helping teachers develop strong character and good judgement in students.

Center for the Advancement of Ethics and Character
School of Education
Boston University
605 Commonwealth Avenue
Boston, MA 02215
Tel: (617) 353-3262
Fax: (617) 353-4351
http://www.bu.edu/education/caec.

The CAEC was founded on the premise that education in its fullest sense is inescapably a moral enterprise and that teachers have a responsibility to support the efforts of parents in the character formation of young people. As the first center of ethics in the country to focus on the education of teachers, the CAEC endeavors to provide an intellectual and practical framework for teachers. To this end, the CAEC sponsors courses at Boston University; conducts research; hosts conferences, institutes, and lectures; and offers consulting assistance.

Center for Civic Education
5146 Douglas Fir Road
Calabasas, CA 91302-1467
Tel: (818) 591-9321
Fax: (818) 591-9330
http://www.civiced.org

The CCE is an educational corporation dedicated to fostering the development of informed, responsible participation in civic life specializing in civic/citizenship education, law-related education, and international educational exchange programs for developing democracies. Programs focus on the U.S. Constitution and Bill of Rights and the rights and responsibilities of citizens. The CCE administers a wide range of critically acclaimed curricula, such as CIVITAS and "We the People—Project Citizen," a civic education project for grades 6–9. The center also offers teacher training and community-based programs.

The Center for Collaborative Education
An Affiliate of the Coalition of Essential Schools
1573 Madison Ave., Room 201
New York, NY 10029-3899
Tel: (212) 348-7821
Fax: (212) 348-7850
http://www.cce.org

The Center for Collaborative Education was formed by a handful of public schools in New York City. With 39 member elementary and secondary public schools, CCE is a school-based advocate for educational change, a facilitator between and within schools, and an initiator of new programs. CCE simultaneously works within schools in the New York City system and is a public voice advocating school change. CCE provides technical assistance and develops research and projects to illustrate the educational practices of student-based education. CCE is part of parent-teacher coalitions to mobilize against budget cuts and other systemwide problems.

Center for Learning
21590 Center Ridge Road
Rocky Road, OH 44116
Tel: (216) 331-1404
Fax: (216) 331-5414
http://www.centerforlearning.org

The Center for Learning supports a growing national and international community of educators by publishing more than 500 values-based curriculum resources and providing a growing list of complementary services. CEL's mission is to develop values-based curriculum materials in English and language arts, literature, and social studies; it engages a network of 400 master teachers in authoring and publishing classroom-tested lesson plans. CEL sponsors in-service opportunities and an English Summer Workshop Series for educators. CEL publishes NOVELNews, a newsletter that provides teaching ideas for integrating values and literature.

Center for the Fourth and Fifth R's
P.O. Box 2000, SUNY, Cortland, Education Department
Cortland, NY 13045
Tel: (607) 753-2455 / Fax: (607) 753-5980
http://www.cortland.edu/www/c4n5rs

The Center for the Fourth and Fifth R's (Respect and Responsibility) serves as a resource in character education. Led by Thomas Lickona, the Center disseminates articles on character education, sponsors an annual summer institute in character education, publishes a newsletter, and is building a network of "Fourth and Fifth R's Schools" committed to teaching respect, responsibility and other core ethical virtues as the basis of good character. The Center promotes a 12-point comprehensive approach to character education, one that uses all aspects of school life as deliberate opportunities for character development.

Character Development Foundation
P.O. Box 4782
Manchester, NH 03108-4782
Tel/Fax: (603) 472-3063
http://www.charactered.org

The Character Development Foundation promotes the character development of children; provides support for character development in schools, at home and in communities; and educates teachers, administrators, and parents in the area of character education. The foundation's principal activities are conducting character education workshops for teachers, parents, and others on such topics as "An Overview of Character Education," "Character Education Through Literature," "Character Education Through Problem Solving," and "Character Education for School and Community." The foundation also has a speakers' bureau.

Character Development Group
P.O. Box 9211
Chapel Hill, NC 27515-9211
Tel: (919) 967-2110 / Fax: (919) 967-2139
http://www.charactereducation.com

Led by Phil Vincent, the CDG offers a range of services, including publications, staff development, implementation assistance, and assessment for character education programs at school sites and in school systems. Dr. Vincent believes that character education must become part of the ethos of a school. His workshops focus on five "Spokes" of character education: Rules and Procedures; Cooperative Learning; Quality Literature; Teaching for Thinking; and Service Learning. He shows educators how to develop character in students without using add-on curriculum; recognize the importance of consistent rules and procedures; develop a multi-year plan that involves all stakeholders; and get results in any learning environment.

Character Education Institute
California University of Pennsylvania
250 University Avenue, Box 75
California, PA 15419-1394
Tel: (724) 938-4500 / Fax: (724) 938-4156
http://www.cup/edu/education/charactered

Directed by Henry Huffman, the CEI provides character education support to school districts, higher education, businesses, and parents; facilitates research; and offers character education graduate work and inservice education. The Institute has three goals: 1) serve as a resource to the university's colleges and departments as they contribute to the moral development of students; 2) provide an outreach to school districts studying or implementing character education initiatives; and 3) prepare education majors and teachers in service for their unavoidable role as character educators.

Character Education Partnership
1025 Connecticut Ave, NW Suite 1011
Washington, DC 20036
Tel: (800) 988-8081 / Fax: (202) 296-7779
www.character.org

CEP is a nonpartisan coalition of organizations and individuals dedicated to developing moral character and civic virtue in our nation's youth as one means of creating a more compassionate and responsible society. CEP serves as a national clearinghouse, collecting and distributing information on programs designed to develop moral character and civic virtue. Each year CEP recognizes exemplary schools and districts through its "National Schools of Character" Awards Program. CEP publishes a newsletter and hosts a national forum to exchange information and further develop effective character and civic education programs.

The Communitarian Network
2130 H Street, NW, Suite 703
Washington, DC 20052
Tel: (202) 994-7997
http://www.gwu.edu/~ccps/

Led by Amitai Etzioni, the Communitarian Network believes that individual liberties depend upon bolstering the foundations of civil society, namely families, schools, and neighborhoods. The network's goal is to change public policies, to affect change in daily practices and social interaction, and to foster and stimulate dialogue. CN publishes frequent articles on character education in its quarterly journal and produces a newsletter. The network also sponsors teach-ins and publishes policy recommendations. The network has organized White House Conferences on "Character Building for a Democratic and Civil Society."

The Council for Global Education
P.O. Box 57218
Washington, DC 20036-9998
Tel: (202) 496-9780 / Fax: (202) 496-9781
http://www.globaleducation.org

The Council for Global Education, a membership organization, offers learning/training materials for parents, teachers, children, young adults, and administrators, including curriculum improvements and innovations information. The Council, led by Sunita Ghandi, has a database of international experts and a networking service where members can exchange curriculum ideas and materials; share innovations, lessons learned, and success stories; and engage in discussion forums.

The Consortium for Social Responsibility and Character in Education
University of Central Florida, College of Education
Suite ED-318, P.O. Box 161992
Orlando, FL 32816-1992
Tel: (407) 823-3819 / Fax: (407) 823-5135
http://ucfed.ucf.edu/csrce

This Consortium has three purposes: 1) to serve as a hub for partnerships for improving the effectiveness of education and networking in social responsibility and character in education; 2) to promote excellence by encouraging research and evaluation on the best practices in character education and law-related education; and 3) to encourage lifelong learning with a focus on improving the development of social responsibility and character in education. The Consortium stimulates research through sponsored studies, graduate fellowships, and workshops. It also serves as a clearinghouse of ideas, information, and materials.

Developmental Studies Center
2000 Embarcadero, Suite 305
Oakland, CA 94606-5300
Tel: (510) 533-0213 / Fax: (510) 464-3670
http://www.devstu.org

The Developmental Studies Center's (DSC) mission is to help children develop intellectually, ethically, and socially. DSC is involved with developing school-based programs; the building of a caring community in the classroom and school; developing after-school and parent-involvement programs; providing professional development services and resources; producing and disseminating educational resources, which includes curricular and instructional materials and staff development materials; and systematically evaluating programs and resources.

Educators for Social Responsibility
23 Garden Street
Cambridge, MA 02138
Tel: (800) 370-2515 / Fax: (617) 864-5164
http://www.esrnational.org

Educators for Social Responsibility's (ESR) mission is to make teaching social responsibility a core practice in education so that young people develop the convictions and skills needed to shape a safe, sustainable, democratic, and just world. A national leader in supporting schools, families, and children, ESR is recognized for its prominent role in social and emotional learning, character education, conflict resolution, violence prevention, and intergroup relations. ESR offers comprehensive programs, resources, and training for adults who teach children at every developmental level, preschool through high school.

Ethics Resource Center
1747 Pennsylvania Avenue, NW, Suite 400
Washington, DC 20006
Tel: (202) 737-2258 / Fax: (202) 737-2227
http://www.ethics.org

The mission of the ERC is to be a leader and catalyst in fostering ethical practices in individuals and institutions. ERC's goals are to inspire individuals to act ethically toward one another; to inspire institutions to act ethically, recognizing their role as transmitters of values; and to inspire individuals and institutions to join together in fostering ethical communities. ERC believes that character education provides strategies and tools to teachers, administrators, staff, students, parents, and community members so that they may create environments in which all children can achieve academic standards.

International Center for Character Education
University of San Diego
5998 Alcala Park
San Diego, CA 92110-2492

Tel: (619) 260-5980 / Fax: (619) 260-7480
http://teachvalues.org

The International Center for Character Education's (ICCE) mission is to enable school personnel, parents, teacher educators, faith community members, youth providers, and concerned individuals to come together to study, discuss, learn, practice, reflect, and write on issues, programs, problems, and promises regarding the character education of children and youth. Some ICCE activities include a Certificate in Character Education program, an on-line training program, a master's degree specialization in character education, yearly academies and conferences, program assessment, publications, workshops, and consulting services.

International Educational Foundation
4 West 43rd Street
New York, NY 10036
Tel: (212) 944-7466 / Fax: (212) 944-6683
www.iefcharactered.org

The International Educational Foundation (IEF) works collaboratively with schools, teachers, and educational leaders throughout the world to promote education that cultivates the heart and character. IEF advocates a multidimensional approach: Character Education, Marriage and Family Education, Abstinence Education, and Drug Prevention Education. IEF has been active in such countries as China and Russia, helping educators respond effectively to the challenges of rapid social transformation. Emphasis on the unifying appeal of universal values helps transcend cultural and national differences.

Jalmar Press
24426 S. Main Street, Unit 702
Carson, CA 90745
Tel: (310) 816-3085 / Order number: (800) 662-9662,
http://www.jalmarpress.com/

The purpose of Jalmar Press is to promote and integrate healthy self-esteem, nonviolent/compassionate communication, stress management, whole-brain learning, and emotional intelligence into the lives of children and their caregivers worldwide so that personal worth, responsibility, and integrity become paramount and commonplace. Jalmar Press was created to provide psychologists, counselors, teachers, social workers, parents, and other caregivers with activity-driven books to help develop the social, emotional, and ethical skills that ultimately lead to academic success.

Josephson Institute of Ethics
4640 Admiralty Way, Suite 1001
Marina del Rey, CA 90292-6610
Tel: (310) 306-1868 / Fax: (310) 827-1864
http://www.josephsoninstitute.org

The Joseph & Edna Josephson Institute of Ethics was founded by Michael
Josephson in honor of his parents to improve the ethical quality of society
by advocating principled reasoning and ethical decision making. Since
1987, the Institute has conducted programs and workshops for more than
100,000 influential leaders, including legislators and mayors, high-rank-
ing public executives, congressional staff, editors and reporters, senior
corporate and nonprofit executives, judges and lawyers, and military and
police officers. The Character Counts! Coalition youth-education initiative is a project of the Institute.

The Kenan Ethics Program
Duke University
Box 90432, 102 West Duke Building
Durham, NC 27708
Tel: (919) 660-3033 / Fax: (919) 660-3049
http://kenan.ethics.duke.edu

The Kenan Ethics Program (KEP) supports the study and teaching of
ethics and promotes moral reflection and commitment in personal, professional, community, and civic life. KEP encourages moral inquiry across
intellectual disciplines and professions and moral reflection about cam-
pus practices and policies. KEP supports efforts to address ethical questions of public concern within and across communities. KEP aims to support creative innovation in the teaching of ethics locally, nationally, and
internationally by promoting approaches that strengthen critical reflection, enrich moral imagination, and inspire personal integrity and civic
commitment.

National Professional Resources
25 South Regent St.
Port Chester, NY 10573
Tel: (800) 453-7461 / Fax: (914) 937-9327
http://www.nprinc.com

National Professional Resources (NPR) is a major distributor of professional development materials to support the nation's teachers in the field
of education. NPR is an organization with a strong background in staff
development and training within the field of education. NPR's mission is
to provide resources to ensure that learners of all ages, with differing

abilities and some at risk, will reach their maximum potential and will meet national, state, and local standards. NPR produces its own videos, distributes books for staff development, and sponsors conferences and workshops throughout the U.S.

School for Ethical Education
440 Wheelers Farm Road
Milford, CT 06460
Tel: (203) 783-4439 / Fax: (203) 783-4461
http://www.ethicsed.org

The SEE promotes ethics in action for the creation of positive character and the advancement of responsible and caring communities. SEE recognizes the need for a focus on sound ethical reasoning in the advancement of ethical behavior within human interactions. SEE provides classes and seminars to educators, parents, student leaders, and community members. It collaborates with school districts, parent organizations, professional education centers, and institutions of higher and continuing education. SEE instructors teach, write, and speak at events and meetings and consult with relevant educational organizations.

Other Associations Supportive of Character Education

American Federation of Teachers, 555 New Jersey Avenue, NW, Washington, DC 20001; Tel: (202) 879-4400, www.aft.org

American Youth Foundation, 2331 Hampton Avenue, St. Louis, MO 63139; Tel: (314) 646-6000, Fax: (314) 772-7542, http://www.ayf.com

Association for Moral Education, c/o Darcia Narvaez, Secretary, College of Education and Human Development, University of Minnesota, 206 Burton Hall, 178 Pillsbury Drive, SE, Minneapolis, Minnesota 55455; http://www4.wittenberg.edu/ame/index.html

Association for Supervision and Curriculum Development, 1703 North Beauregard Street, Alexandria, VA 22311-1714; Tel: (800) 933-ASCD, Fax: (703) 575-5400, http://www.ascd.org

Association of Teacher Educators, 1900 Association Drive, Suite ATE, Reston, VA 20191-1502; Tel: (703) 620-3110, Fax: (703) 620-9530, http://www.siu.edu/departments/coe/ate

The Boyer Center, Messiah College, Harrisburg, PA 17027; Tel: (717) 796-5077, Fax: (717) 796-5081, http://www.boyercenter.org

Center for Youth Citizenship (CYC), 9738 Lincoln Village Drive, Sacramento, CA 95827; Tel: (916) 228-2322, Fax: (916) 228-2493, http://www.clre.org

Close-Up Foundation, 44 Canal Center Plaza, Alexandria, VA 22314; Tel: (703) 706-3330, Fax: (703) 706-0001, http://www.closeup.org

The Committee for Children, 2203 Airport Way S., Suite 500, Seattle, WA 98134-2027; Tel: (800) 634-4449 or (206) 343-1223, Fax: (206) 343-1445, http://www.cfchildren.org/reachus.htm

The Jean Piaget Society, Department of Human Development, Graduate School of Education, Larsen Hall, Harvard University, Cambridge, MA 02138; http://www.piaget.org

Learn and Serve America, Corporation for National Service, 1201 New York Avenue, NW, Washington, DC 20525; Tel: (202) 606-5000, http://www.cns.gov/learn/index.html

Learning for Life, Boy Scouts of America, 1325 West Walnut Hill Lane, PO Box 152079, Irving, TX 75015-2079; Tel: (972) 580-2000, http://www.learning-for-life.org

National Education Association, Suite 800, 1201 Sixteenth Street, NW, Washington, DC 20036; Tel: (202) 833-4000, http://www.nea.org

National School Boards Association, 1680 Duke Street, Alexandria, VA 22314; Tel: (703) 838-6722, (703) 683-7590, http://www.nsba.org

National Youth Leadership Council, 1910 West County Road B, St. Paul, MN 55113; Tel: (651) 631-3672, Fax: (651) 631-2955, http://www.nylc.org

Northeast Foundation for Children, 71 Montague City Road, Greenfield, MA 01301; Tel: (800) 360-6332, Fax: (413) 772-2097, http://www.responsiveclassroom.org

Phi Delta Kappa International, 408 N. Union St., P.O. Box 789, Bloomington, IN 47402-0789; Tel: (800) 766-1156, Fax: (812) 339-

0018, http://www.pdkintl.org

The Sangreal Group, 1309 Linda Vista St., Suite 80, Orange, California 92869; Tel: (800) 598-7073, E-mail: psbowen@sangreal-group.com

Southern Poverty Law Center, 400 Washington Ave., Montgomery, AL 36104; Tel: (334) 264-0286, Fax: (334) 264-3121, http://www.splcenter.org

Youth Service America, 1101 Fifteenth Street, NW, Suite 200, Washington, DC 20005; Tel: (202) 296-2992, ext. 43, Fax: (202) 296-4030, http://www.ysa.org

Notes

[1] From "I Have a Dream" by Martin Luther King, Jr., a speech delivered on the steps of the Lincoln Memorial, Washington, DC, on August 28, 1963.

[2] V. Neufelt, ed. *Webster's New World Dictionary*, 3rd ed. (New York: Simon and Schuster, 1998), 235.

[3] *Aspen Declaration on Character Education*, The Josephson Institute of Ethics (Aspen, CO: July, 1992). http://www.charactercounts.org/aspen.htm

[4] T. Lickona, *Educating for Character: How Our Schools Can Teach Respect and Responsibility* (New York: Bantam Books, 1991), 51.

[5] *Aspen Declaration on Character Education.*

[6] K. Ryan, "The New Moral Education," *Phi Delta Kappan*, 68 (1986).

[7] H. Kirschenbaum, *100 Ways to Enhance Values and Morality in Schools and Youth Settings* (Boston: Allyn and Bacon, 1995).

[8] D. Berreth and S. Berman, "The Moral Dimensions of Schools," *Educational Leadership*, 54 (1997): 27.

[9] P. London, "Character Education and Clinical Intervention: A Paradigm Shift for U.S. Schools," *Phi Delta Kappan*, 68 (1987): 671.

[10] E. DeRoche and M. Williams, *Educating Hearts and Minds: A Comprehensive Character Education Framework*, 2nd ed. (Thousand Oaks, CA: Corwin Press, 2001), 24–25.

[11] J. Leming, "Character Education and Multicultural Education: Conflicts and Prospects," *Educational Horizons*, 72 (1994): 123.

[12] J. Stratton, *How Students Have Changed: A Call to Action for Our Children's Future* (Arlington, VA: American Association of School Administrators, 1995).

[13] K. Ryan and K. Bohlin, *Building Character in Schools* (San Francisco, CA: Jossey-Bass, 1999), 18–24.

[14] P. Glanzer, "The Character to Seek Justice," *Phi Delta Kappan*, 96 (1998): 435.

[15] Taken from E. DeRoche and M. Williams, *Educating Hearts and Minds: A Comprehensive Character Education Framework*, 2nd ed. (CA: Corwin Press, 2001); and E. DeRoche and M. Williams, *Character Education: A Guide for School Administrators* (Lanham, MD: Scarecrow Press, 2001).

[16] DeRoche and Williams, *Character Education.*

[17] DeRoche and Williams, *Educating Hearts and Minds*, 52–63.

[18] N. Noddings, "Teaching Themes of Care," *Phi Delta Kappan*, 76 (1995): 675.

19 G. Maeroff, "Alter Destinies: Making Life Better for School Children in Need," *Phi Delta Kappan*, 79 (1998): 427.

20 J. C. Fenald, *Standard Handbook of Synonyms, Antonyms, and Prepositions* (New York: Funk & Wagnalls, 1947), 142.

21 Public Agenda (2000). www.publicagenda.org

22 DeRoche and Williams, *Educating Hearts and Minds.*

23 DeRoche and Williams, *Educating Hearts and Minds*, 118–19.

24 National Parent Teachers Association, *National Standards for Parent/Family Involvement Programs* (Chicago, IL: Author, 1998).

25 S. Covey, *Principle-Centered Leadership* (New York: Summit Books, 1991), 19.

26 J. Leming, *Character Education: Lessons from the Past, Models for the Future* (Camden, ME: The Institute for Global Ethics, 1993).

27 Child Development Project. http://www.devstu.org

28 News Item, *Education Week*, 64 (1999).

29 J. Dewey, *Problems of Men* (New York: Philosophical Library, 1946), 90.

30 *Proverbs*, 22:6.

31 R. Coles, *The Moral Intelligence of Children: How to Raise a Moral Child* (New York: Random House, 1997), 31.

32 M. Williams, "Actions Speak Louder Than Words: What Students Think About Character Education," *Educational Leadership*, 51 (November 1993): 23.

33 M. Williams, "Actions Speak Louder than Words: What Students Think About Character Education," *Educational Leadership*, 51 (November 1993); and J. Leming, "Applied Ethics or Character Education?: Contrasting Approaches to the Development of Moral Teachers" (paper presented at the annual meeting of the American Association of Colleges of Teacher Education, Chicago, February 2000).

34 K. Bosworth, "Caring for Others and Being Cared for," *Phi Delta Kappan*, 26 (1995): 686–93.

35 Coles, *The Moral Intelligence of Children*, 178.

36 M. D. Merrill, "Constructivism and Instructional Design," *Educational Technology*, 1 (May 1991): 45–53.

37 J. G. Brooks and M. G. Brooks, *In Search of Understanding: The Case for Constructivist Classrooms* (Alexandria, VA: Association for the Supervision and Curriculum Development, 1993): Chapter 9.

38 J. Dalton, and M. Watson, *Among Friends: Classrooms Where Caring and Learning Prevail* (Oakland, CA: Developmental Studies Center, 1997), 172.

39 Leming, *Character Education.*

40 Lickona, *Educating for Character*, 138.

41 Ryan and Bohlin, *Building Character in Schools*, 239.

42 M. Watson, "Classroom Control: At What Price?," *Teacher Education Quarterly*, 11 (Autumn 1984).

43 Leming, *Character Education.*

44 Kirschenbaum, *100 Ways To Enhance Values and Morality In Schools and Youth Settings*, 92.

45 B. McEwan, *The Art of Classroom Management* (Upper Saddle River, NJ: Merrill, 2000), 197.

46 Ryan and Bohlin, *Building Character in Schools*, 105.

47 Lickona, *Educating for Character*, 287.

48 D. W. Johnson and R. T. Johnson, *Reducing School Violence Through Conflict Resolution*

(Alexandria, VA: Association of Supervision and Curriculum Development, 1995).

[49] R. D. Enright, "An Integration of Social Cognitive Development and Cognitive Processing: Educational Applications," *American Educational Research Journal*, 17 (Spring 1980): 21–41.

[50] Lickona, *Educating for Character*, 288–89.

[51] Johnson and Johnson, *Reducing School Violence Through Conflict Resolution*, 29.

[52] D. W. Johnson and R. T. Johnson, *Cooperation and Competition: Theory and Research* (Edina, MN: Interaction Book Company, 1989).

[53] D. W. Johnson, R. T. Johnson, E. J. Holubec, and P. Roy, *Circles of Learning: Cooperation in the Classroom* (Alexandria, VA: Association for Supervision and Curriculum Development, 1984).

[54] Lickona, *Educating for Character*, 186.

[55] Coles, *The Moral Intelligence of Children*, 182.

[56] M. Herczog, "Service Learning: Meeting Content Standards by Serving the Needs of the World," *SUNBURST* (February 2000): 20.

[57] L. S. Wiley, *Comprehensive Character-Building Classroom: A Handbook for Teachers* (DeBary, FL: Longwood Communications, 1998), 182—183.

[58] S. Jeroski, "Finding Out What We Need to Know," in A. Costa, J. Bellanca, and R. Fogarty (eds.), *If Minds Matter: A Forward to the Future*, Vol II (Palatine, IL: IRI/Skylight Publishing, 1992), 281.

[59] DeRoche and Williams, *Educating Hearts and Minds*, Chapter 6; and DeRoche and Williams, *Character Education*, Chapter 9.

[60] K. Burke, *How To Assess Authentic Learning* (Arlington Heights, IL: Skylight Publishing, 1999), 72–73.

[61] R. Sagor, *How to Conduct Collaborative Action Research* (Alexandria, VA: Association for Supervision and Curriculum Development, 1992).

[62] The Character Education Partnership, *Character Education: Questions and Answers* (Washington, DC: Author, 1995), 4.

[63] Ryan and Bohlin, *Building Character in Schools*, 95.

[64] Wiley, *Comprehensive Character-Building Classroom*, 135–36.

[65] P. F. Vincent, *Developing Character in Students* 2nd ed. (Chapel Hill, NC: Character Development Publishing, 1999), 101.

[66] Vincent, *Developing Character in Students*, 103.

[67] E. A. Wynne and K. Ryan, *Reclaiming Our Schools: A Handbook on Teaching Character, Academics, and Discipline* (New York: Merrill Press, 1993), 156.

[68] A. Harless, unpublished materials titled *Character Education Curriculum*, University of San Diego (Fall 2000).

[69] M. H. Loew, unpublished materials titled *Character Education Curriculum and Program*, University of San Diego (Fall 2000). The program integrated into Loew's curriculum plan is the *Building Esteem in Students Today* (BEST) program.

[70] *Building Esteem in Students Today* (BEST) program. Information about BEST was taken from the Web site at http://www.bestprogram.org.

[71] *Building Esteem in Students Today* (BEST) program, http://www.bestprogram.org.

[72] Lickona, *Educating for Character*, 180.

[73] P. Ravin, unpublished materials, including *RUSD Academic Content Standards for History/Social Science K–12* (5/99), 1.

[74] Ramona Unified School District (RUSD) *Resources for Character Education* (Author, September 13, 1998), 10–11.

75 R. Kanaby, "Willing Learners Remove Apathy from the Equation," *The High School Magazine*, 4 (1996): 9.

76 J. Holloway, "Extracurricular Activities: The Path to Academic Success?" *Educational Leadership*, 57 (1999): 87–88.

77 L. Lisy-Macan, Principal, Brookside Elementary School, Binghamton, NY in *Schools of Character: The 1998 Award-winning Schools* (New York: McGraw-Hill, 1998), 5.

78 Ms. Friedman, health teacher, Buck Lodge Middle School, Adelphi, MD in *Schools of Character: The 1998 Award-winning Schools* (New York: McGraw-Hill, 1998), 7.

79 J. M. Bower, Principal, Benjamin Franklin Classical Charter School, Franklin, MA in *Schools of Character: The 1998 Award-winning Schools* (New York: McGraw-Hill, 1998), 3.

80 Lickona, *Educating for Character*, 395.

81 DeRoche and Williams, *Educating Hearts and Minds*, 113.

82 B. Rutherford and S. Billig, "Eight Lessons of Parent, Family, and Community Involvement in the Middle Grades," *Phi Delta Kappan*, 76 (1995): 68.

83 H. R. LeGette, Parents, *Kids, and Character: 21 Strategies to Help Your Children Develop Good Character* (Chapel Hill, NC: Character Development Publishing, 1999), 5.

84 Lowell Joint School District (California), *Character Education Program Manual*, 6.

85 W. Ribas, "Tips for Reaching Parents," *Educational Leadership*, 56 (1998): 83–85.

86 A. Baker, "Improving Parent Involvement Programs and Practice: A Qualitative Study of Teacher Perceptions," *The School Community Journal*, 7 (1997): 27–55.

87 LeGette, *Parents, Kids, and Character*, 5.